Adda Blanche Doughty Brookhart

MEMORIES

COMPILED BY
DONALD RAY BROOKHART

outskirts
press

Outskirts Press, Inc.
http://www.outskirtspress.com

ISBN: 978-1-9772-5691-1

PRINTED IN THE UNITED STATES OF AMERICA

Dedication:

This book is dedicated to my father, Harry Adrian Brookhart and to all Brookharts—past, present, and future.

Table of Contents

Introduction

COLORADO IS WELL known for two things: the chain of "fourteeners" dotting the majestic Rocky Mountains and the gold rush of 1859. However, Colorado owes much of its history to the pioneers who settled the eastern plains. It was not the beautiful peaks, nor the gold rush, that drew the hardy folks to settle the Kansas and Nebraska Territories that eventually became the State of Colorado. It was the good soil available for farming and ranching. While the beautiful mountain peaks remain, the gold rush that initially brought over a hundred thousand people to the region was over in the blink of an eye. Within a few years, placer mining in Colorado's Front Range had been virtually exhausted. Settlements were left to the ghosts as many of the '59ers, financially ruined, returned home. The wealthier prospectors had mainly come from the East Coast, but most of those who worked the granite and streams were from prairies south and east of the Territories. Some from each population remained to lode mine. Most who remained in Colorado didn't settle in the mountains or in the foothills; they headed to the eastern plains, still the "Kansas Territory," to join emigrants who came, not in search of gold or scenery, but for the good farming soil and cattle ranching.

When she was a little girl in 1886, my grandmother, Adda Blanche (Doughty) Brookhart and her family traveled from Missouri to settle "the west," the eastern plains of the newly minted State of Colorado. Adda's story makes it abundantly clear that these families never expected to strike it rich. These pioneering families knew that hard work and harsh living conditions awaited them. They brought grit, courage, and faith with them in their covered wagons, for they knew *these* things would be more valuable to them than gold.

My name is Donald (Don) Ray Brookhart. I was born on January 31, 1942, in Lamar, Colorado, to parents Harry Adrian Brookhart and Irene May Orr. Adda Blanche Doughty Brookhart was my father's mother, my grandmother. My roots remain on the eastern plains, where Adda's withered before she died in Pueblo, Colorado, in 1946. She died after a long battle with illness when I was still very young and, while I do not have strong memories of her when she was living; her memory lives in each of her descendants. She was a strong, creative, intelligent, and successful woman. These traits she passed on to her ancestors.

My father, Adda's son, worked the last farm that my grandparents lived on and had built into the Brookhart Nursery west of Las Animas. Many of the trees lining the streets of Las Animas today were purchased as saplings from my grandparent's nursery. I lived in this area until I met and fell in love with Marie J. Vanderpoel; we married in 1971 in Gold Hill, a small town nestled in the foothills above Boulder, Colorado. After retiring, we moved from southeastern Colorado to Gold Hill, and I have lived here ever since. This place, too, is brimming with history—but that is a story for another time. Gold Hill was one of the first mountain settlements that resulted from the '59er Gold Rush. That said, my heart and soul remain on the eastern plains where my ancestors lay buried.

Like Adda Blanche Doughty Brookhart and her son Lester Raymond Brookhart, I had planned to write my story. I find that my tenure as the family archivist is drawing to a close. I am writing down these few facts for my family—past, present, and future—and for any readers interested in the history of the eastern plains of Colorado. For now, I turn this narrative over to abler storytellers than I: Adda and Lester.

Adda wrote of her impressions and adventures as a little girl traveling with her family in a covered wagon to the eastern Colorado plains to build a sod home and farm. It is a beautifully written piece that emphasizes the simplicity, hardships, and joys of that time. Lester's story is robustly told as an autobiography that includes a treasure trove of historical facts about the Brookharts and his own life as a witness to WWI, WWII, the Spanish Flu, and other events of the time.

They say a picture paints a thousand words, and to that end, you will find photos of the Brookhart family in Appendix 2.

Introduction to Adda's Story

ADDA BLANCHE DOUGHTY Brookhart wrote "*...an account of my experiences as I remember them.*" Like many Brookharts born before and after Adda, she wanted to leave stories of the past for her descendants. Adda was born on May 4, 1878. Her story is centered on her journey as a young girl from Nodaway, Missouri. She was part of the first wave of emigrants to the eastern Great Plains of the newly minted state of Colorado. Her father, Benjamin Franklin Doughty, had been advised to seek a higher, drier climate to improve his tuberculosis. Stories had been circulating about the dry climate and prairie lands available after the US Government had forcibly removed the Indians. The federal government was offering acreage free of charge to those willing to homestead it. The decision was made to take his wife, Rachel Katherine Birchfield Doughty, their five children (one still a babe-in-arms), and his younger brother to claim and settle the land.

In 1886, when Adda was just eight years old, she, four of her siblings, and her mother stayed behind in Nishna Botna, Missouri, with her grandmother while her father, her oldest brother, and her uncle departed to stake their claim on the vast prairie lands. She recounts a delightful summer spent waiting for news that land had been secured in the west. Her father sent for them, and after a long ride in a covered wagon, she arrived on the banks of the Republican River. The landscape was completely alien to her as the nearest town, Hugo, Colorado, was nearly forty miles away. She was used to having schools, churches, neighbors, and doctors nearby. Her family, after some hiccups, set about building a sod hut near what is today known as Flagler. In her beautifully written story, we have a ringside seat as a deserted, sod-house dotted prairie transforms into a bustling town complete with a railroad. Buffalo and cowboys roamed the prairies, typhus and other fevers claimed loved ones, and the land was plowed and ranched. With her story, Adda reminds us that while they were deprived of many material goods and services, there was always an abundance of love, gratitude, faith, innovation, and courage.

Adda's story ends somewhat abruptly, and there is little doubt among her descendants that she had intended to write more. And, we are poorer for not having more of her words, for she was articulate, well educated, and wrote beautifully. Her story leaves off where she is still a girl, though she hints at her future as a teacher. While any other accounts she may have written are lost to history, we are fortunate to have recovered many of the poems she wrote throughout her adult life. These rhyming poems written in the classical style are reminiscent of Emily Dickinson and John Donne. Her poems blend intelligence and reason with passion and beauty; she evoked times past with themes present for most of us today. She writes of intense grief after her son died in an accident and of the joy, she experienced as she saw field lilies on a trip to California. These poems, and others, are included in Appendix 1.

The young woman who spent a lifetime teaching school on the prairies, who fell in love and married Henry Brookhart, and who raised seven children did not include these events in her memoir. That she had been elected as County Clerk for two terms and helped her husband run a nursery in Las Animas was also not included. These stories continue to be told by her relatives and descendants through the years around supper tables and front porches. Some of her story is picked up by her eldest son, Lester, who wrote an autobiography in the late 1960s. His autobiography is included in the second half of this book.

Prior to publication, both Adda's and Lester's manuscripts were reviewed by myself and professionally edited. Care was taken to make no changes other than to correct some punctuation and obvious typing errors and to clarify terms and geographical locations that may not be familiar to the modern-day reader.

Memories of Pioneering Days of 1886

AS THE WHEELS of time slowly, surely, silently, majestically move onward, changes so great are taking place. Such changes come so slowly as to be almost imperceptible. A life of fifty, sixty or seventy years is only such a little space of time when compared with the immense eternities that have passed and are still to pass. The sorrows, hopes and fears, as well as the modes of living, thinking and doing things are quickly forgotten from one generation to the next.

Because of my desire to leave to my children and grandchildren some little idea of things as they were during my span of life, I have undertaken to write an account of my experiences as I remember them.

It takes many and varied experiences to shape a life, and although the road for some must be lonely, rocky and rough, for others it may be a path of beauty, health and happiness, or so it seems. We cannot know the inner life and what would make for spiritual development in one would not do at all for another.

My own life has been of the first type. I have had a strenuous, busy, storm-strewed life.

Fate left me, one May morning in 1878 a tiny little mite of a girl in a little farm home on the banks of the Nod-a-Way[1] River in Missouri,

---

1   This refers to what is currently called the Nodaway River that runs through western Missouri and east of the Missouri River.

near Maryville. I was the daughter of Benjamin and Rachel Doughty. When I was about four years old, we moved to Nebraska, where I grew to the age of four when I started school at Johnson, Nebraska.

Memories are dim, but prominent among the memories that linger are: a delicate mother, three brothers, and two sisters and a happy home. There were trees, birds, a garden, flowers and the love of a delicate, brooding mother. My father was away from home a great deal of the time.

Then a great change came into the home. My father became tubercular (contracted tuberculosis). His strength was ebbing away and we felt that something had to be done. The family discussed over and over about various plans of action.

It was decided that we should seek a higher and drier climate since this was believed to be beneficial for a tubercular condition. Scores of people were discussing the new West, where there was plenty of free land awaiting the coming of new settlers. It was the land of "great resources and opportunities.

I remember hearing my father and mother discussing the subject. Father earnestly talked about the land on which no one had yet lived, where millions of acres were waiting to be homesteaded. Mother objected because there were no schools, churches, towns and railroads. At last she was persuaded to undertake the long journey to the vast unknown.

So the house was sold, all the household effects were parted with, except the most necessary articles. The space which would carry the household goods was limited to the space in two covered wagons. The two covered wagons and teams were purchased and plans were made for the journey.

All this was very exciting for me and my brothers and sisters for we had never traveled much before. We were very happy at the prospect of a long trip. So we bade our old life and friends goodbye and started our journey. We crossed the Missouri River in a ferry boat to a little town called Nishna Botna,[2] Missouri, which had been my father's boyhood home.

Some thirty years before this, my grandfather and grandmother, Sampson and Elizabeth Doughty, seeking a new home, had left their parents' home in Kentucky in a covered wagon and braved the trackless wilderness of forests and rivers, seeking this new home in Nishna Botna, where there would be better privileges for their families. They had homesteaded a tract of land. Sampson Doughty had edited a newspaper in Johnson, Nebraska during the "bloody" days in Kansas of Civil War days. I had often visited here with my parents as a young child.

This home is still a very wonderful memory to me. I can still see my grandmother's two- story white frame house with beautiful old trees all about, with a green velvety lawn, with its white picket fence and latchet gate and flower garden. There were roses, lilacs, tiger lilies, sweet Marys, bachelor's buttons, butter and eggs, and four o'clocks. I always marveled at the four o'clocks because of their habit of closing at sun down. There was the old orchard with gnarled old apple trees, peach trees, pear trees, cherry trees and grape vines. All this beauty made its silent appeal to me when I lay on the soft green grass, gazed at the piles of white fleecy clouds floating overhead and breathed the fragrance of the wonderful flowers.

One big tree extended over the house and from my bedroom window upstairs I could see right into the little birds' homes and watch the feeding of the young. One day a bird flew right into my bedroom. I found that it was building a nest in my grandmother's black riding skirt that she had worn to ride her Kentucky saddle horse. Across the road from my grandmother's home lay a hill pasture of 30 or 40 acres. To

---

2   Today, there does not exist a town called Nishna Botna. The Nishnabotna River is a tributary east of the Missouri River. The name comes from the language spoken by the Chiwere tribe (also called the Iowa-Otoe-Missouria) that inhabited the region. The word means "canoe-making river." (Wikipedia, *https://en.wikipedia.org/wiki/Nishnabotna_River*).

me this was a wonderful fairyland of stately old trees, grapevines and flowers.

At last the time came when my father was to start toward the West to find us a new home. He and his brother, John Doughty age 23, and the oldest son, Frank, were to start with the two covered wagons and locate a home. My mother, brothers, and sisters were to stay with my grandmother and travel by train to the new home later. At last the morning arrived when the trip was to start. We were up very early finishing the last details of packing the two covered wagons. The white canvas tops were all clean and new. Articles of clothing and food were stored in the wagons for the long trip.

I had noticed my grandmother furtively wiping her eyes on her checkered gingham apron. The horses were stamping and fighting flies, impatient to be off. As they leaned forward, the harness creaked and the wagons began to move forward. We watched until they passed from sight. In our childhood innocence we wonderingly scanned Mother's and Grandmother's faces, now so covered with tears at the parting. For were not we, too, to soon be leaving for the wonderland "out West"? The "West", where Indians, cowboys, coyotes, mountains and other exciting things would be part of our new life. At least this was the idea we had gleaned from stories we had heard about the West.

Slowly and sorrowfully, Mother and Grandmother, carrying the ten-month-old baby, Myrtle, returned to the old home to wait and wait for letters or news of the westward-bound travelers. Little did we children realize what fate had in store for us; what hardships were awaiting us in this unknown, unsettled home-to-be. Mail service was poor and the letters that came were few and far between and not very encouraging. While passing through western Kansas they had visited an aunt in Roaks County and had laid over for a week to rest up, clean clothes, and get a new food supply.

The summer we stayed at my grandmother's home was a great

landmark in our lives. My sister, "Mollie" (Mary Elizabeth) was twelve years old and I was eight years old. We had lived in a small town in Nebraska and attended school there (before moving to my grandmother's home in Missouri). We liked to read, and to write little plays and act them out. We took turns reciting "Paul Revere's Ride", "Curfew Must Not Ring Tonight", "I Stood on the Bridge at Midnight" and similar poems. Sometimes our programs were changed to "camp meetings." We took turns conducting the services, prayers and all. Our grandmother thought this was a terrible waste of time and sacrilege and thought we should be learning to cook and sew. Our mother, who had been a teacher, rather sided with us girls. She had been a teacher in private schools in Nebraska City in the early days.

What a pity our grandmother could not understand that each generation was changing; each had a mission to perform and we were to become some of the pioneers of Colorado as our grandparents had been pioneers before us in Virginia and Kentucky.

The golden prairies of the West must be settled and a living wrested from them. We must have courage, hardihood, originality and initiative. We were to find that water was scarce, rainfall was scant and there were few trees for building material. Our grandparents had found all these things plentiful in Virginia and Kentucky when they settled there. In Colorado, only the most courageous, hardy and persevering settlers became permanent.

My sister and I had exchanged some old junk to a "rag man" and had received some bright tin cups. We begged permission to "strip" the cows of a dairy herd nearby. This meant the getting of the last few drops of milk left by the milkers. We put this milk in the tin cups. We strained the milk through a clean white cloth. We then constructed a little cellar, covering it with a clean cloth, barrel staves and dirt. We decided to keep the milk in the cellar, make butter and sell it as we had seen our grandmother do. However, the cows stepped on our cellar and put an end to our plans.

We immediately set out on a new adventure. In the backyard of the farm house, about thirty feet from the kitchen door, stood an immense box elder tree. Its gaunt limbs reached eagerly skyward and spread heavy green branches on every side. It was so large it would have taken three or four grown people holding hands to circle its big trunk. Our eyes spied out its possibilities at once. My sister proposed a play house in the tree, fixed securely in its sheltering leafy green arms, far from prying critical adult eyes. It would be a retreat where all sewing, knitting and various disturbing things might be left safely behind while we dreamed over story books and fairy stories, or talked over possible future wild adventures with Indians and cowboys in the misty and distant far away Colorado. We began to wonder how our plan could be accomplished. It would be necessary to wait until Grandmother was away. One day she went to market at the neighboring village. This was our chance. She had harnessed the old family horse, Dexter, and hitched him to the buggy. She finally drove away with many urgent commands that we get busy and keep busy and behave until she returned. We immediately climbed the tree after procuring a hammer, saw, nails and boards. Soon there was the *rip rip rip* of the saw. Nimbly and quickly the boards were firmly nailed to the big limbs and a railing fashioned about two feet above the floor to keep us from stepping or falling off while reading our books. Such necessities as paper and pencils were brought from the house. All debris such as twigs and sawdust were carefully swept away and all tools were returned. When our grandmother arrived home, we were innocently sitting in the living room industriously sewing.

We had, by this time, become skilled climbers and as soon as dinner was over and the dishes washed we would, while unobserved, silently climb to our tree house. Here we would tell stories or read. The noise of the leaves in the wind was sufficient to drown out our whispers. After tiring of the retreat we would watch for our chance and silently slide down and enter the house in some other direction, much to our dear grandmother's bewilderment. For several weeks all went well. Then one day we had been helping to gather some little pear-shaped tomatoes for preserving. We carried a can full to our retreat and were sitting eating them and reading when my sister noticed grandmother come under the tree, feeding her little chickens. My sister hurriedly reached over to touch me to warn me that our position was critical. In so doing she overturned the can of tomatoes and they came pouring down about our grandmother's head to our dismay and her consternation. Our little dream of freedom was now only a burst bubble. Our grandmother went upstairs and looked through the window and saw our place of concealment.

All this was immediately presented to our mother in its fullest details. We were immediately whipped, our faces scoured, our hair combed and we were put to work, sewing patchwork quilt blocks. We were warned against any future repetition of any such escapades. I think for at least two hours we felt conscience-stricken and were sorry that we had sawed the big tree and wasted precious time. But childhood is not capable of lasting impressions and the very next day we were seeking new worlds to conquer. We began studying some field of escape from the terrible monotony of making quilt blocks. We stole away and went to the little attic where we explored salt barrels filled with ears of popcorn, strings of dried green beans, piles of homemade soap, bunches of dried herbs to be used as medicines, an old bird cage, an old loom and spinning wheel. We found a very old trunk with wedding gowns yellowed with age, dried flowers which had been on some loved one's casket. We saw a rope that figured in a hanging. A number of men of the family had avenged the murder of a relative after securing incriminating evidence of guilt.

I remember my grandmother telling of an incident when she was a young girl in Kentucky. This incident must have happened about 1835. Her grandmother was about twelve years of age. A big dance was being held at her home. Since it was summertime, the huge fireplace was filled with fragrant boughs. Her brother, a young man of twenty-two years, was at the dance with his sweetheart. Grandmother hid behind the evergreens in the fireplace. Her brother and sweetheart paused in front of the fireplace to plan an elopement for that very evening and she heard all the details. Later in the evening, when there were inquiries about the couple's absence, she was the only one who knew that the elopers had ridden horseback through the hills to a Presbyterian minister and had the ceremony performed, then joined the merrymakers at the dance again.

About this time, we received a letter from my father telling us that our father had arrived in Colorado, selected a homestead of 160 acres, a tree claim of the same acreage and was going to drive to Denver to file on the land. The land selected for the homestead was about 2 ½ miles east of where the town of Flagler now stands. My father sent us train fare for the family to make the trip.

We immediately began making preparations for the trip. The plans were for us to stay at the home of my Uncle Bill Christian, who lived in the town of Nishna Botna. The next day my mother, two brothers Jim and George, two sisters Mollie and Myrtle, and I took the train for the West. On the morning of August 26, 1886 the train stopped at Hugo, Colorado, the nearest railroad town to our new home. My father was there to meet us. Our covered wagon was awaiting us. We were all very excited to actually see the west with its Indians, cowboys, etc. that we had heard so much about.

Our father was very enthusiastic about the possibilities of the new land but our mother regretted that they were so far from schools and doctors. The homestead was on the Republican River about forty miles from Hugo and about eight miles from the nearest neighbor. Great herds of long-horned cattle grazed on the rich buffalo grass. We also saw herds of antelope, as many as a thousand in a herd. There were many patches of cacti and we children often got the needle-like thorns in our feet.

Finally we arrived at the homestead and Father showed us where the house was to be built, the orchard to be planted and a cave. For awhile we lived in the home of a man named Simon Rumming while our house was being constructed. Simon Rumming was a cowboy and, true to western custom, welcomed any travelers into his home.

Buffalo grass sod was the only building material available. The covered tops of the wagon were removed. Boards were then placed on the running gears to form a level place on which the sod was to be placed. The best sod is that in which there are plentiful grass roots and was found in valleys where water had stood and where the soil was not sandy.

The spot was selected by Mother for the new home. Near it was a low bowl-shaped spot called a lagoon. The ground was sunken and had apparently been trampled by buffalo. My brother, Frank, had a buckskin pony which he rode back and forth between the new sod house and the home of the cowboy. Construction of the new house was rushed for we would soon have winter. The rectangular pieces of sod were carried and put in place much as a brick mason builds a house. A level was used constantly to keep the walls straight.

The house contained two large rooms with a sod partition between them. Later we added a lean-to kitchen.

Mother wrote letters to friends and relatives in Missouri which had to be carried forty miles to be mailed.

August soon passed. September days were beautiful, but quickly passed also, and no school, or signs that there ever would be. We were the only family in the neighborhood with children. Mother began to worry about it. We had brought some books and these were unpacked, and read and re-read. No newspapers or magazines. It seemed so very strange. Mother often looked sad and weary and discouraged but I and my sister had climbed every hill, turned over every rock we could lift and tore off our aprons, filling them with rocks to carry home to show Mother. We had explored every cave or hole we could find, and were longing for an Indian attack or something to happen. As our brother monopolized the pony now, going hunting, we were envious and longed for new adventures.

One lovely September day a stranger rode into the yard, apparently to water his horses, he was riding one and leading one, a pack horse loaded with a small tent, bedroll and other bundles. Here, indeed, was material for new thought. He asked a few questions where we were from. How long we had been here? How long would we stay in the house? We very eagerly told him our father was building a new house not far away, then we added a profuse lot of extra information, asked about 100 questions, and at last he escaped and rode about one-half mile up the valley, out of our earshot (probably because of the questions) unsaddled his horse, set up his tent, unloaded the packhorse, fixed his bed and was apparently going to stay awhile. He was a rather short, sandy-haired man, with blue eyes, dressed in the usual fashion of that day, perhaps with "chaps" or long leather leggings worn over his other clothes. In his outfit was a long-range rifle. I remember he was the soul of kindness and good humor. We found his name to be Simon Rumming and that the house we were in belonged to him also. After getting his camp all neatly arranged, he took a sharp spade going about a mile above to where some cool, crystal springs gushed and bubbled from between some large rocks and down the hillside forming itself into several deep ponds. Here he began digging a ditch, which in reply to our numerous anxious questions, (we having followed him) he explained it would be an irrigating ditch to carry water over the land to make crops and gardens grow. As soon as we had gleaned all the information he seemed willing to give, without us using too much persuasion, we immediately left him at his work, and flew home to impart the news to Mother and the rest.

He had come home from the fall round-up and had intended to work on and improve his ranch. He never mentioned us vacating his house and gave us such valuable information and helped us in many ways.

About the middle of October, the sod house was finished and ready for the roof, window and door frames, and a floor but the latter could be dispensed with and the dirt floor the answer for awhile. The lumber must be hauled from the distant railroad station where we had met the wagons before. The roof was first covered with heavy tar paper, then heavy sods laid over it, and then several loads of dirt, gravel or sand applied to keep the terrible wind storms from carrying it away.

The men took the wagons and teams and journeyed to Hugo and procured the materials. There was a townsite about six or seven miles further down the river called Hoyt, but it failed to materialize. Some journeyed to Haigler, Nebraska for supplies, but our men chose Hugo.

Soon the home began to look more like a shelter. The roof was on, the window casings in only one full window, the other half size, to economize. The front door was hung and from some cliffs nearby, the men procured a sort of plaster or native lime and were making ready to plaster the interior walls, which were now merely the edges of sods with grass roots sticking out and tiny clods of dirt hanging to them, which were dislodged at every little jar, and showered dust and dirt about tables and beds. But one evening my uncle John Doughty, about twenty-three years old, was taken severely ill with temperature, chills, weakness and no way to obtain help. My mother bathed him, put a cold compress to his hot forehead, gave physic and various home remedies but he grew rapidly worse. He had made the long journey from Missouri and had been feeling bad for several days before this attack. His fever grew higher and he was at times delirious. Drinking water had been very hard to obtain, sometimes from the river or springs and there was no way to obtain any kind of fresh fruit, or vegetables. I remember my mother making him gruel, or well-cooked porridge, and doing all she could think of, but to no avail. He became feverish and delirious and so my father decided he must try to get him to the town of Hugo and get advice from a doctor and different water, food and some better way to care for him. All the family were greatly troubled at his illness, for our dear grandmother, Uncle John's mother, was far away in Missouri at the little farm waiting, watching and praying that her dear boys so far away might be successful in finding new homes and sending for her, so all faces were so sad and all hearts heavy.

The old covered wagon was again re-assembled the top and bows being replaced, the bed springs put back in, the bed covers and ticks put back on again and Uncle John, burning with fever, and talking about his mother and home, in his delirium, was carefully lifted into the bed on the wagon and the driver instructed to drive very carefully and slowly. My father drove a buckboard and team. I do not know where he had obtained them, perhaps borrowed from some near-by ranch. I went with him in the buckboard. We were to hasten on ahead of the slow covered-wagon and make what preparations we could. About half way between the homestead and the town of Hugo, Colorado was a large cattle ranch owned by a Mr. Ketchum and a Mr. Pugsley, so called the K.P. Ranch. The ranch house was a frame building with an upstairs and a cellar beneath it. With substantial barns and granaries, immense corrals and branding chutes.

Just before reaching the ranch, we met a large, heavy-set man in a new top buggy and driving a fine span of trotting horses. We stopped to talk, as any and all travelers did at that time, for meeting fellow travelers was such a rare thing at that time and usually the need for information was mutual. My father quickly outlined the situation, telling of the covered wagon with the sick man which was following us, explaining the very serious condition of the young man and the urgent need for help and medicine. Our new acquaintance proved to be Mr. Pugsley, one of the owners of the ranch ahead, who had come from Kansas City on an inspection trip, having several thousand cattle grazing the prairies around about the ranch.

He seemed much concerned and anxious to help us and he advised that my father stop the wagon at the ranch and carry my Uncle John to a bed in the ranch house. He said that perhaps he had what they then called "mountain fever", but what I think now is called ty-phoid fever. This advice was very welcome and was carried out. The rest of the family was sent for and we were soon established tempo-rarily in the old ranch house and a doctor obtained, but it was too late. The disease was too far advanced and one night in the lonely old ranch house, calling "Oh, Ben, let me get up and dress. There's Mother at the gate" who he seemed to be able to see, although we knew her to be hundreds of miles away in Missouri, perhaps praying for her boy, he died. We stood a saddened, lonely little group about the rough home-made bed with bowed heads.

Then duty called. Trips had to be made to Hugo, messages sent, one to his mother and others to other relatives, all in Missouri. Clothes had to be cleaned and made ready, meals must some way be gotten and ate. The ranch owner was very kind and helpful, urging us to stay on for the winter at the ranch and cook for the cowboys. We were to receive 25 cents per meal and have fuel and house furnished free.

Soon my grandmother arrived, all worn out and broken hearted at the loss of her baby-boy, the last left at home of a large family. The little funeral group wended its way to Hugo and burial was made near there. Grandmother returned to her home, lonely and sad, leaving her beloved son in a grass covered grave, I believe about the first to be buried there (See photo, Appendix 2).

Mr. Pugsley, now about ready to return to his home in Kansas City, again urged us to accept his offer and stay during the winter at the old ranch, urging that it would be so much better for us being only twenty miles from the railroad and about forty miles away from our home-stead. Winter was at the door, fuel was a serious problem, my father's health was so poor as well as six small children who might need medi-cal help. At last, at Mother's urging, we decided to stay and return in spring to the unfinished sod house and homestead. At best it was a sad and lonely time, but we had not expected "a bed of roses" on this wild, untamed prairie.

Winter set in early that year. Cold, blustery stormy days sped by. No newspapers, telephones, or radios. About the only amusement was hunting antelope, rabbits and ducks, all of which were present in great abundance. Some days were fuller and happier than others, especially when Mother baked cookies or made doughnuts or we were perhaps taken along on a hunting trip and left with the buggy, while the men saddled ponies and galloped away over the buffalo grass-covered prairies.

Life was so different from Nebraska or Missouri with no neighbors nearer than 20 miles, no means of getting in touch with the outside world except long, wearisome dusty trips made to Hugo. As we were told the roads would soon be impassable for wagons on account of snow drifts, we had to lay in a supply of necessities.

Every few days, a cloud of white dust afar off would perhaps be a forerunner of a bunch of cowboys with big cowboy hats, chaps, booted and spurred, with revolvers and ammunition belts and sometimes rifles. They would ride up, dismount and ask us to prepare dinner or supper or perhaps they would be there for several days. They were employed by the ranch owners to look after the thousands of cattle, brand calves, watch for cattle rustlers and keep the owner informed about all the affairs at the ranch. They were a jolly, happy-go-lucky lot of fellows, and excellent shots and expert riders. Well do I remember once making up a bed some of them had slept in and finding a large, heavy, loaded revolver under the pillow. I was afraid to touch it and called Mother to come at once. Tough and daredevil though they might be, when alone or with other groups of men, they were kind, gentle and mild mannered when coming in the society of women and children. But I expect when away on the range or with other bands of cowboys, they were perhaps as "wild and woolly" as the cowboys of modern fiction and the "movies."

The big roomy kitchen in the ranch was equipped with a large cast-iron cook stove, and a long home-made pine board table covered with a dark colored oilcloth. A stairway led from the kitchen to the upstairs bed rooms. In the living room on the first floor in an opening out of the kitchen was a large, tall old-fashioned cast heating stove. A combination writing desk and cupboard filled one corner. At the other corner were built-in bunks or beds, one above the other, three in all, made of pine boards and innocent of springs. They were upholstered in straw ticks. I don't know where the straw came from. It might have been prairie hay. I have read that, in a similar ranch house, George Pullman got his ideas for the modern Pullman sleepers which were first used in 1856.

It was in one of these crude beds that my Uncle John had passed his last few days of fatal illness. All the bedding had been washed and now the bunks had become the beds of parents and the smaller children. I remember that along about Christmas time I was sleeping in the upper berth, and looking across the top of the high bookcase I discovered a few packages that I knew must have recently been brought from Hugo. Afterwards, they were found to have been some candy and nuts which had been bought and stored away for safekeeping until Christmas, which as it afterward came about, came to be the last Christmas our family circle remained unbroken. As I write this nearly fifty years later, with Father and Mother both gone and my eldest brother and all the others scattered so far apart, that I needs must think that the Christmas spent in the old ranch house must have, in many ways, been a happy time as we were then all together.

But to return again to the description of the old ranch, the barns were much nicer in every way than the house. They were very large and capacious with box stalls and a large well-made harness and saddle room and feed rooms. I remember one large room was filled with large bottles of medicine for stock, linseed oil, turpentine, coal oil and a ton or more of leaf tobacco, jugs, kegs, stacks of curry combs and brushes, piles of saddle blankets and dried cow and sheep hides and many other things. Above this part was a large haymow filled with hay.

I suppose it was native hay, cut along the creek, on the banks of which the ranch was located.

Above this, and reached only by a ladder and door which was kept padlocked and the key carried by the owner of the ranch and accessible only to him, was a large "pigeon house" with little separate nests or houses and scores of beautiful birds of multi-colored plumage, wheeling and cooing about in the bright sunshine and uttering little domestic sounds inside their little homes. The owner, Mr. Pugsley, was very proud of his pets and every time he visited the ranch, coming on the train from the city to Hugo, he never failed to bring something especially for the pigeons—some new foods or appliances for the nesting houses—and sometimes he would seem to be extraordinarily jolly and well-pleased with his bundles and boxes, and usually it turned out he had brought several pairs of some rare new kind of birds. On these occasions he would unlock it, and after giving us children a sly, jolly wink, he would warn us not to try to follow him, but watch for the fine new birds he would turn loose. To us it was all a grand treat, and sometimes the new birds would tumble over and over. He called them "tumblers." All the other birds, some very beautiful, would circle in ever-widening circles and gurgle in soft throaty love notes. Sometimes our "pigeon Santa Claus" would stay for an hour or so with his pets. They had no fear of him and loved him dearly and would settle all about his shoulders and arms talking soft, sweet pigeon talk. The ranch was well stocked with many other fowls including several pairs of pea fowl, proud, haughty and strutting about with wide spread, beautiful tails, flocks of squawking guineas, calling in loud, raucous notes—*pot-rack, pot-rack*—to be heard far above all other barnyard noises, and several varieties of ducks and chickens.

The corrals were especially large, spacious and well-built and seemed to be staunch enough to stand the sudden onslaught of the most vicious horses or cattle. They were built of long, smooth poles like telegraph poles. I cannot remember any barbed wire. Barbed wire came into use in 1861. It came in various sizes and was constructed for different kinds of livestock. Some must have been for sheep as they were much lower in height, and there was a large number of sheep pelts in the barn. There were a large number of branding irons, made with different letters or designs as J_J, K-P-J, or O-O, each ranchman having a different brand to mark his cattle to tell them from other ranchers' stock. They had a narrow crate-like affair called a branding chute. The animal to be branded was crowded, pushed and punched along until fast-wedged, then a red-hot iron containing the selected brand was applied to the flesh on hip or side. The hair sizzled, the flesh was burnt. It was all very cruel it seemed, but was the only device for marking, except slitting the ear. Branding was done in spring just before turning loose the big herds on summer range.

Some of the highest, strongest-built corrals were called roping corrals where they ran in the wild, prairie-bred range ponies and broke them for saddle horses. Many a day found us children perched on the roofs of adjacent sheds when we knew the cowboys were planning to rope and break horses. With bulging eyes, skinny hands and legs clutching the roof, we witnessed some terrible battles when some particularly wild-eyed mustang came plunging, pawing and kicking into the enclosure, after having been chased by the mounted cowboys racing like the wind across the prairies, gradually closing the circle, trying to break through but all to no avail. The mounted cowboys were very skilled in this game, and with foam-flecked nostrils, fiery eyes, and flowing manes and tails and ever-ready heels, the horses defended their freedom, only at last to find themselves in the strong, high corrals and the skillfully thrown lariat settling in circles about their necks or sometimes their heels.

The thrills we enjoyed were equal to any now caused by the modern movies. It was all very exhilarating and Mother's call for dinner had very little effect on us, secure on our perch, as long as these wild-west dramas were in progress.

After the capture, the taming began. A specially contrived halter, called a "hackamore" was adjusted to the head and nose. Some of the riders had a way of holding to the hackamore and the tail of the bronco and whirling them about until they fell from dizziness, then slapping on the saddle while they were still lying on the ground. Then letting him struggle to his feet, the cowboy sprang into the saddle and away went the wild mount, uncertain as to what it all meant. He would buck, pitch, run and sometimes let out an awful sound like a cow bawling. Aside from these thrilling exhibitions and our daily household affairs, things moved very slowly and monotonously. Occasionally a freighter wagon or perhaps a train of several traveling together came through. Most of these came from Haigler, Nebraska and were traveling southwest into New Mexico, perhaps to Santa Fe.

Occasionally a settler from forty-five to fifty miles back on the prairies would camp for the night. Some were hauling large double sideboard loads of the bones of cattle and buffalo which they had gathered from the prairie or below an embankment where they had drifted in fierce storms. These could readily be sold at Hugo. They were sometimes sent to New Orleans to use in the manufacture of molasses. A large load would bring about $3.00 or $4.00 and the money used to purchase flour and syrup, brown lump sugar, green coffee to be roasted and ground at home, salt and other necessities like matches, coal-oil, lamp flues, etc.

Only the barest necessities of life could be obtained by the early settlers or at least a great many of them. After seven or eight lean years, it was better and times not quite so hard, but what we call hard times in 1935 would have been untold wonders and plenty. We would have been astonished at the wonderful array of modern luxuries and good things to be secured and enjoyed in those times. I believe people have been spoiled by too many fine useful, helpful things and perhaps a lesson might be necessary to give them a better way of appreciating their blessings. As I look back through the mist of memories of fifty years, one stands out plainly. The memory of a father, mother and six children sitting around a long, homemade table, covered with dark oilcloth, some fluffy brown-crusted biscuits, a large platter of meat and a big dish of gravy – a dish of stewed prunes, some molasses in an old-fashioned molasses pitcher, water to drink, fond looks from parents to children, love to parents beaming from happy, young eyes and a very happy, contented family—even with very little worldly goods, and almost no money, but as yet an unbroken family circle. Alas, it was soon to be different.

Winter, by December, had set in earnest—cold, snowy, blustery days and every few days an unusually frigid wave of cold. My father's lung trouble, which all through the warm, sunny summer and fall had improved steadily, now began to take on an aggravated form.

His grief and depression was an aggravating cause too, as his brother, John, had been the baby of a large family of children and his mother's despair when she returned to the old home alone was constantly in his memory. He had several hemorrhages from his lungs, and at last was forced to take to his bed for most of the time. For Mother it was a hard, trying time—so far from neighbors or help of any kind. It was such cold, stormy weather and Father was so ill in bed. There were six children, three boys and three girls, one a baby about a year old who was our household pet. Her name was Myrtle and she had large, dark eyes and dark hair.

Of course wash days were frequent and conveniences lacking. One day in the midst of a large washing a sudden storm began to gather. The wind swung to the north and turned extremely cold. At once my mother wiped her hands and flew to look for the two small boys, George who was about four years old and James about two. They had wandered away from the house and were following single file, just the shoulders and heads visible, what they called "tattletails" which were deeply worn cow trails. Then all at once, after glancing anxiously about, we heard her calling them and started to run across the prairie after them. We could see approaching from the north a large herd of Texas longhorn cattle. They were bellowing and running before the oncoming storm.

My mother, brave and without a thought for herself, never stopping to slip on a coat or wrap up in any way, and just leaving the steaming tub of wash, flew to her little boys like the wind. Seizing one under each arm, she began to return despite being a slender, frail little woman. On came the cattle and it looked as though she would be overwhelmed and trampled to death, but finally reached safety, although completely exhausted. Soon the blizzard broke in all its fury of whirling, white snow and icy wind, but we were all snug in bed and comfortable. The next morning Mother was quite ill, but dressed and managed to somehow cook and feed and care for the hungry family.

Soon, however, she was compelled to return to bed as the storm raged on. Soon she had a raging fever. My father did all he could think of to allay her suffering but her fever grew higher and higher. We children tried to care for the baby, who was not weaned yet, trying to get her to suck some nourishment from small pieces of steak or bread crusts. She cried and cried to go to Mother, who by this time was growing delirious and even though so desperately sick was fighting against the suggestion of my father, who wanted to send my brother Frank, just fifteen years old, through the storm to Hugo for a doctor. She'd say "Oh Ben! Please don't send my boy out in this storm, he'd surely freeze!"

But Father decided to try to get help some way, so began to wrap and bundle him in all the warm things he could find, wrapping his legs in layers and layers of gunnysack cut into strips and with many forebodings and without Mother's knowledge, we lost sight of him amid the whirling snowflakes. As the storm had grown more and more fierce and he was riding a small cow pony, Father had given him many instructions as to the road and the necessity of not getting lost in the storm. Soon even the fence posts became almost invisible because of being crusted with snow. We children stood about the cook stove in the kitchen trying to soothe Myrtle, the baby girl. All through that tense, terrible day the storm roared on and night descended on the old ranch house, with Mother steadily growing worse. There was no news from my brother, Frank, no medical help and a great, thick flurry blanket of snow enwrapping everything about. The wind tore and pulled at every loose board or shingle. We got what we could to eat, clustered in the old kitchen around the little cook stove. The baby was wrapped in a blanket and fed what we could find. At last, she fretted herself to sleep.

My father stayed right by Mother's bed with a pale, terror stricken face. He tried all the old home remedies, poultices, plasters, hot irons, cold compresses on her head for fever and everything else he could. All night he kept vigil. Sometime in the night we children crept up the stairs and into bed, carrying the sleeping baby, leaving her by her bedside, weary and dead tired. We slept soundly to wake to look out at a new world. A great, glistening white blanket covered the earth it seemed—some places four or five feet deep. My brother had not returned, nor had we heard from him, so we could only wonder, fearful for his safety. About eight o'clock my mother called my oldest sister, Mollie, to her bedside and told her, "Mollie, I am going away. I will have to leave you. Be a good girl and take good care of all of the children, especially little Myrtle." She then asked for the baby to be given to her. Father placed her in her arms. Then she began to gasp for breath. My father took his large, brimmed, felt hat and began fanning her with it, but she was soon gone and as we stood about the rude bunk, sorrowing until my father, overcome with it, called us into the kitchen and closed the door. Here we were grouped until a knock came on the door. On opening it a man staggered in, utterly exhausted by the long struggle he had made through the terrible storm. He, too, was on a journey to Hugo to call a doctor for a neighbor's wife. He had already come about twenty-five miles. He was driving a one-horse cart and carried a long pole for sounding the depth of drifts.

Seeing the little group huddled about, he inquired of my father as to the cause of his grief. My father told him of our second great loss. He was so sorry about it all and spoke of the terrible roads and no medical aid. After warming and drinking some hot coffee, he continued on. His name was Al Hendricks, and he lived in Seibert for many years after this. We heard that when he had procured a doctor and returned home again, he found the neighbor's wife had died too, as did many of the pioneer women. (Many years after this, I met this man in Billings, Oklahoma where I had moved when I left Colorado and we talked about the big storm.)

About noon of the next day a sleigh drove up. In it were two men, a woman dressed in woolens and wrapped in buffalo robes with hot bricks packed about her feet. My brother was with them. It seems the man, Hendricks, had told them about the conditions so they brought some jugs of sweet milk and some canned milk, medicine and various other things. The jugs of milk were frozen solid. They were soon put in hot water to melt. The woman cuddled the baby and cried over her and asked to adopt her. My father had now taken to his bed with a hemorrhage in his lungs caused by the storm and the loss of our mother. It looked like as if he, too, might leave behind a family of children. As different people came in after a few days, his answer to all questions about anyone taking any of the children was "after I am gone. I am fighting now to live to raise them."

The casket was brought from Hugo, a black walnut casket with bright handles and lined with silk and lace about the edge. The little woman who had come in the sleigh dressed Mother in her very best dress and they laid her in the casket. I remember, now, after fifty years have sped away, just how sweet and dear she looked to me and how much I missed her all the following years and do yet. The weather was entirely too bad for us to go to Hugo. So, watching tearfully, we saw them take her away to be buried next to our Uncle John, who had so recently left us. Years later I found the two mounds which are now in a pasture, the rest of the cemetery having been moved to a new location.

Now it became necessary for my sister and me to take up the burden of caring for the rest of the family. She was twelve years old and I between eight and nine. My father was confined to his bed most of the winter and managed in some way to get along. The winter dragged slowly by, and with the coming of spring weather, Father's health began to improve and my baby sister had learned to drink canned milk. The Doctor advised that we get the baby out into the sunshine and air. As we had no baby buggy or any other way to get her about, we took turns carrying her. Although we found it a hard, dispiriting job, we took our turns willingly. Soon she could eat well enough and became strong enough to run about quite well.

Life began to be complicated for us, without Mother and with so many pressing duties about the house—taking care of the baby, and cooking and dishwashing. Father had written to our grandmother asking her to rent out the old home farm near Nishna Botna and come west to live near him as he was in very critical condition at that time. On account of his tubercular condition, she had consented but it would take some time to sell things and rent the place.

As we needed milk so badly and there were literally thousands of cows, many with young calves and large udders, all about us on the prairie, Mr. Pugsley, the ranch owner, suggested after looking over the number of children who needed milk, that we try breaking in a cow or two. He said he would give them to us and take then to our homestead, if we succeeded in the enterprise, and he sure hoped we could. So a likely young cow, with a newborn calf with very wobbly legs, was selected and run into the branding chute. She was securely tied to insure safety and then they tried to milk her through the spaces between the poles at the side. She bawled, struggled, strained at the ropes and bars, fell down, plunged up and in fact did all she knew in cow-lore to discourage them. But, the cowboys looked at the baby and three year-old Jim and grimly milked on, emptying it from a pint cup each time into the pail. After awhile they joyfully came bringing a pail full of creamy looking milk to the house. Oh! My, how good it was and the little ones "swigged it down" and the milk gravy for supper, Yum! Yum! The next day and every day for about two weeks this milking program was carried out in the same energetic way. It took my big brother and three or four cowboys to complete the operation each time. Then feeding the calf too was a great adventure, not at all to be sniffed at, for the calf too was a range-bred longhorn, and felt its breeding. But after what seemed about a month, if counting the terrific exercise and all, it submitted to sucking a finger submerged in a pail of milk, in lieu of the way nature provided. This day was indeed a red-letter day for the cowboys, who seemed very jubilant. But, the cow still had another card up her sleeve, so to speak, and refused to eat or drink in confinement and finally they turned her loose in a small lot. At once she ran and jumped the fence, fell down, scrambled up and was away like the wind, never to return and even deserted her calf, which left in a milkless world, must now be fed on a paste made of flour, meal and water until it too got away and followed a big herd of rangers and was lost.

We tried the same procedure with two more cows, but always the cows came out ahead and we finally gave it up. The winter wore away slowly, and as the warmer days brought lots of sunshine my father became a lot stronger. The boys and men planned several big antelope hunts and I often was allowed to accompany them. There were large herds of them which frequented the prairies near the old ranch. Sometimes it looked like there might be as many as a thousand in one herd. They were a beautiful tan color with white tails, and on the slightest alarm ran like the wind, soon outdistancing the swiftest horse. The only chance for antelope steak we found lay not in finding the antelope but with a long-range rifle, and a good huntsman with a quick, sure shot. The antelope kept guards or pickets standing on the higher slopes, apparently to give the alarm at the approach of men with guns, which they had some way of detecting, perhaps by the odor. The main herd would graze in the valleys and behind hills until the outposts dashed with them to safety, but although we succeeded in getting only a few, our friends the cowboys often had good luck and divided with us both ducks and rabbits which were also plentiful. Sometimes the hunters would kill a mother antelope and leave a little one, only a month or so old, which the hunters would catch and bring home and feed on cow's milk and it was not unusual to ride up to a little sod prairie home to see these graceful little pets playing about.

But now the big drifts of snow had melted and the roads were getting passable again. Father began to take more interest in things and made plans to return to our claim and finish the sod house which we had left so hurriedly when Uncle first became sick. Grandmother was soon to return to us, and we must get back and finish and occupy the new home. So, the covered wagon was again packed and we began the return trip home. It was located at a point which is now about two and a half miles east of what is now the town of Flagler, but as there was no railroad through this country at that time, nor any towns or people or anything, we just followed the old trails that led in the direction we must go. After a long, jolting tiresome trip, we again arrived at our claim and began to prepare it as our home by plastering it with native lime, setting up stoves and putting in what little household belongings we then owned. Father made bedsteads from boards and also tables, cupboards and many other little things that were necessary.

We found we now had some neighbors, a man and wife, four girls and boy, who had recently arrived from Texas with a covered wagon and an ox team and had taken up land on the Republican River about two miles from where we lived. We soon became acquainted and were fast friends for many years. The name of this family was Strode. The girls were Ellen, May and Stella [3] and the boy's name was

---

3   Adda does not list the name of the fourth girl in her memoir.

William. Some of them still live near Flagler. The mother and father passed away years ago. Other families began to come now and then with wagons, a few implements, horses and a few chickens tied on in a coop. There were no fences and everybody staked or hobbled their horses. To hobble meant to tie the front feet together so they could eat but not run away.

One family I remember so well were named Lind, and a little girl my age named Mabel Lind was my seat mate at the first school at Crystal Springs sod school house, and suddenly became very ill and died. She was buried among the very first in the Flagler Cemetery.

A family by the name of MacDonald came too. They had a boy named Frank that I remember. There was also a man and wife named Lyons accompanied by a daughter, Florence, and a grandchild named Archie. These also took land east of Flagler near the Republican River. A man named Charlie Farr, then unmarried, settled a little farther up the river; then a family of McCauleys arrived and a Mr. Dimmet.

I cannot remember the exact time but about three or four years after we came, a great event—great in many ways—took place. The Rock Island Railroad began to build through this community on its way to Denver, Burlington, Flagler, Seibert and more settlers also came and developed into little prairie towns. The railroad proved a great blessing to this isolated little community, for now cattle, sheep and horses could be shipped east and provide an income for settlers, as well as building materials, groceries, drugs and, best of all, mail every day instead of weeks between times. This railroad passed near our home about one mile from us. The excitement ran high at first as we thought the town would be about two miles east of its present location.

At first they talked of naming it Bowser, in honor of an old bachelor who lived there all alone in a little claim shack, with only a dog for company. He was rather an eccentric old fellow and had his dog eat at the table, sleep with him and was quite silly about him in every way. The dog was the sole subject of most of his conversations and many the joke passed about slyly concerning this wonderful dog.

All now was bustle and excitement. The advance crews of pile drivers, scrapers and bridge builders proved to all that it was not simply a dream or a western mirage, but an honest-to-goodness railroad— just exactly what we all wanted and needed. Along with these events, arrived a Mr. Lavington and his young wife. He soon was making an earthmoving scraper fly and tents were erected. A Mr. Will Leeper and his wife, Mary, came and erected a large tent for a place to feed the workmen. Soon a little village grew into being and it became a very busy place. My father kept us away from the camp as he knew it was not for children's amusement, but one fine morning after Mrs. Leeper came, he told me I could go and visit her awhile. I enjoyed it very much and Mrs. Leeper was very kind and nice to me. There were lots of scrapers, mules, wagons, harnesses, men, piles of kindling from the new bridges, lots of flies, and tents for beds and storage. The steady pound of pile drivers were to me a seven days' wonder. Some nearby springs had been dug out, cleaned out and were now in use for a water supply. Some of the men were ill from drinking all kinds of water as they travelled along. They inquired if we had any buttermilk to sell. I eagerly promised to bring some down to the camp each day I churned. (By this time some tamer cows had been acquired some way, but I cannot remember where.) So, each churning day I brought all I had to the work train and it was eagerly drunk by the thirsty men. Then they would collect up nickels and dimes and wrapping them in some paper, would throw them off to me from the flat rail car they rode on.

So, in after years I have always claimed a part in the building of the Rock Island Railroad for I surely furnished the buttermilk. Another nice feature of railroad building that I found was the piles of kindling and short round blocks sawed from the piles when they had to be sawed off. These made useful stools to take the place of chairs. The smaller pieces made excellent kindling, as about all the fuel we had to cook with or to warm ourselves by was called "cow chips." They were merely the sunbaked and dried droppings of the cattle and made a very fair kind of fuel, except for the large amount of ashes it left after burning. Many and many a load of these have I helped gather and pile into a wagon, sometimes even with sideboards on it. They were then hauled to our home and piled somewhere convenient to the house. We also gathered loads of bones, dried and whitened by the sun. These bones had been left by the slaughter of big herds of buffalo by the early hunters who only took the hides off for sale, leaving the rest to waste. Sometimes we would find a whole load beneath a cliff—where big storms had driven both buffalo and cattle over the brink to their death—-the back ones pushing on the leaders until they piled up, killing many. These bones we hauled to Hugo which brought three or four dollars a load, which was a very large load. It was not much pay, but it was money that bought flour, brown sugar, molasses, coffee (green berries which we browned in the oven in a bake pan, then ground in a coffee mill), so different from the vacuum sealed cans we buy now which are roasted and ground and ready to use.

Eastern people began to come very fast after the railroad was built through to Denver. The little town of Flagler was plotted off and a few small frame houses built. Mr. Lavington built a one-room store carrying groceries. Later he built on more room and added dry goods. A Mr. J.W. Augustine and his wife came. They were young married people and afterward he became the County Superintendent of Schools of Kit Carson, Colorado and I received my first certificate to teach in Kit Carson, Colorado during the time he occupied that office. My first certificate was a third grade certificate dated December, 1893 when I was fifteen years old. Later they raised the age to 18 years.

Almost every day more covered wagons came lumbering in, and little soddys began to dot the prairies, a family of McCauleys, several girls who later became school teachers, Annie, Ruth, Effie, LaVerne, were the given names of some of them. A family named Hunt came also. John and Sarah White started a store in town, their nephew

George ( ) and family came with them from Kansas, I believe. Ed Weller, as yet unmarried and quite a sophisticated easterner arrived and was later married to Alice Bishop and they still make Flagler their home along with numerous children and grandchildren. South of the railroad were the H.W. Browns, Millers, Eppersons, Verhoeffs, a family named Stark.

Farther east down the Republican River, were the families of Roses, Braffords, Hendricks, and many others I cannot recall.

All of the people were of sturdy pioneer stock and came determined to make the best of whatever came to pass. They were looking for permanent homes, were rich in courage and determination and with a consuming desire to own their own home. The women were brave beyond belief, having been taken from all the things they had become accustomed to, leaving their old homes, friends, relatives, churches, schools and medical aid. With Spartan courage they burned their bridges behind them to follow and serve their loved ones, husbands and families, with faces turned steadily toward the golden West to do or die, which many in fact did, without ever seeing the "old Eastern home" again, with great purpose and love as a guiding star. In some ways, I could never fully understand how the little sod houses and dugouts became cozy little houses. The walls were plastered and whitewashed or papered with newspapers and rag carpets while rugs, fashioned by loving, though toil-roughened Mothers hands, covered the floors.

Somehow slips of geraniums, chrysanthemums, ivy and fuchsias found their way here, perhaps through the mail, from eastern friends and every sod home soon had big deep windows filled with blooming plants. They flourished tremendously. It seemed that in some way they understood that love was trying to soften the hardships and add a little beauty. Never in wealthy or green houses have I seen more beautiful specimens than those that grew there in the homes of early pioneers.

Books were scarce, a few brought from the old home in the east, a Bible, some McGuffy Readers, a few spelling books, histories or treasured books of poetry or fiction were all that survived the drastic elimination of "un" necessaries, when packing the wagons for the long, long trail. These books were cheerfully loaned back and forth and served as the only source of reading material at that time.

But somehow the law of compensation was all the time silently working for the things they had sacrificed and the hardships they so cheerfully endured. Many worthwhile things were substituted. All the family was drawn closer together in the bonds of loyalty and love, a sort of sacredness of home ties, divorce was unknown, drunkenness and crime almost entirely absent. Children were taught from babyhood the better ways of cleanliness, of character and uprightness, by their parents. Bibles were in almost every home and read in many homes by the parents to their children, as schools and churches were still in misty formation as yet, like many other things.

The books to be procured were read and re-read and thoroughly mastered. They usually went the rounds of the entire neighborhood. The "prodigality of the press" as we have it today—with great dailies, Sunday editions, magazines and libraries was also still in the dim mist of the future. A newspaper was a thing to be kept for weeks and many of the articles, sermons and stories furnished the evening's amusement for an entire family by being read aloud by some member. And when the usefulness of the newspaper was at last at an end, and a new one had come, the old ones found a last resting place on the walls of the lean to or summer kitchen, here to be read and read again by the children, that is, if they hadn't been pasted upside down. Even then I have seen children trying it, and myself once suffered a very lame, stiff neck trying to read all about Consuela Vanderbilt's wedding when she married some Duke in England with great pomp, fuss and feathers[4].

---

4   The New York wedding of Charles Spencer-Churchill (aka, 9th Duke of Marlborough and cousin to the future British Prime Minister Winston Churchill) to American

If they could only have seen the future so swiftly approaching with telephones, radios, moving pictures, talkies, autos, diesel engines and aeroplanes [sic], but it was not yet time. Great blessings in the form of inventions come slowly and always a humble, clean, common man has been selected to bring them or to be the instrument by which the knowledge is given. They are God's richest plans and thoughts for his earthly children and should belong to all alike—rich and poor— and not be seized upon and commercialized or used to augment the "Eternal Evil" which is already on earth in large measure, caused mostly by the greediness of man. Social affairs were composed of whatever we could find to do without money or price. There were taffy pulling parties, the taffy candy usually made of molasses boiled until thick and sticky enough to pull with greased hands and then laid in long strands to cool, to be served later with refreshments—perhaps doughnuts and coffee or cake. The young people played games. "Spin the Platter," "Fruit Basket," and "Heavy, heavy hangs over your Head," could be played inside. "Happy is the Miller Boy" and "Marching down to old Quebec" and "Old Dan Tucker" needed a big moonlit yard and bunch of healthy, happy young people to make a success of what might have been a dull time inside the house. The parents and older people carried on a lively conversation inside, talking about "back home" or "the East" and planning the best way to manage "out here in the West" which they hoped soon to be duplicates of their eastern homes.

Sometimes an itinerant preacher would happen along. It mattered not what denomination or creed. This big open country with its magnificent distances and snow-capped mountains gave a depth of feeling and a wider breadth of view and greater grasp of God's plans and requirements for his people. Ideas that would have died before if born in a crowded eastern environment, here flourished because of these conditions.

So after it "got about" that a "meetin'" was to be held at some

heiress Consuelo Vanderbilt in 1895 commanded headlines for nearly a year.

farm house, every wagon filled with men, women and children as soon as supper could be hurried through, and perhaps a few hymn books hunted up. The men shaved and at least put on clean shirts and maybe blacked their boots. (If they were out of shoe polish, a stove lid, covered with soot was turned over and some vinegar poured over it and a small, woolen rag was used to apply it to the boots, and they took on a beautiful color and shine.) The women put up their front bangs the night before on little strips of tin (cut from some soft tin and covered with paper), and full, ruffled shirts were all pressed out, and bonnets were dusted and perhaps had a bit of new ribbon added. Soon they were rattling merrily over the prairies, making a new road, or following the old trail, to the meeting place. We found long boards and boxes all about the ends and sides of the largest room and soon the meeting was in progress. My, how good it seemed to hear the old songs, such as "Rock of Ages, Cleft for Me" or "We Shall Come Rejoicing, Bringing in the Sheaves." For the children, they played "Little Children, Little Children Who Love Their Redeemer, are the Pure Ones, are the Bright Ones, His Loved and His Own."

Then the minister opened with a prayer. The Bible was read and a sermon preached and more of the old songs which have cheered and comforted down the years were sung. These were followed by "good nights" as everyone bundled into the wagons to go home again, with happier hearts and a feeling way down in our hearts that the same power that had cared and watched over us in our homes far away was indeed present here, and would care for us in the same way here.

Another kind of social affair were the dances usually held in homes until Flagler could boast a new schoolhouse. With a dance hall upstairs, everybody of all ages gathered and the fiddlers played way into the early morning with a stop from twelve until one for a midnight supper. A real feast was sometimes given at the Flagler Hotel. One of the proprietors I remember was a William Keegan with a wife and a son, named Harley. The parlor boasted an old-fashioned organ and while one table was eating, the late comers would gather about it, someone would volunteer to play and the singers would make the old songs ring. Some popular songs at that time were, "Hot Time in Old Town", "Two Little Girls in Blue," "The Little Rosewood Casket of Letters,"[5] "Fair Charlotte," "Shadow of the Pines," "Sweet Bunch of Daisies," and many others.

They all returned to the hall and danced until two or three o'clock before the dance broke up. Then the ones on horseback galloped away and the buggies went spinning home, some with heavy hearts if their "best girl" had danced with some rival too much.

By this time several years had rolled by and the prairies were being conquered in a way. It was hard to make any money however. One morning after I had cleaned up the sod house, I decided to walk down to the railroad camp for a pail of water from the newly opened springs. I heard someone talking of a young man who had come into the camp only a few days before looking for work. He had become very seriously ill they said and was no better. It made me think of Uncle John and my Mother, so I went to hear often of him. I found that he was quite delirious and would roll off his pallet and under the tent wall and on down the hill. They would, of course, bring him back to his bed, but he was too sick to know what he did. My heart was touched and I went sadly home, carrying too much anxiety for a child.

Later in the evening, I heard he had died and they had no way of knowing how to find his people, so he was buried inside the railroad right-of-way. His name was "Silcoin" so that name was carved on a heavy, wooden plank and my cousin John Doughty often gathered the beautiful spring flowers which were so abundant, especially during the rainy seasons. We would carry armfuls to his grave and cover it and sit and talk sorrowfully about his death and wonder if his people ever found out about it. Perhaps he had a little sister or brother

---

5   Written in 1870, the original song was called "package of old letters" often referred
    to as "Little Rosewood Casket." (secondhandsongs.com)

somewhere waiting for him. His untimely death left another sad place in my childhood and until I left Colorado, I never forgot the flowers for him.

About this time, Eastern people began writing to my father to ask if he would plow the ten to twenty acres required by law and plant it to trees. This was required at that time for tree claims. As we needed the money quite badly, he wrote them that "of course he would." He was getting quite well now. I would go with him to cook and wash dishes and drop the tree seed in black walnut they had sent. I, too, would pack and unpack. Often we encountered rattlesnakes and killed them. Sometimes I'd find one coiled about a little bird's nest and the mother flying frantically about, uttering piteous calls. Then a battle ensued. I'd throw dirt on the snake, look for something to smash its head, and however I could, "hold the fort" until my father's arrival from the long furrow around the ten or twenty acres of land. Once a big rain fell and I quickly put everything in under the cover of the tent and took shelter myself as the rain fell in great slithering sheets. Soon, my Daddy arrived, soaking wet and chilled, as these prairie rains were preceded by intense heat and then followed by a big drop in the temperature.

He changed to dry clothes, and as soon as the water ran away to lower ground and the sun came out, we left the shelter of the tent to look about. To my surprise, I found sort of a cross between a fish and an animal. It had legs, and could walk after a fashion. Where they came from I never knew. I found one on top of the tent. Later I heard them called "water puppies"[6] That night the ground in the tent was quite damp, but we spread a wagon cover of canvas, doubled and folded down first and we were quite comfortable. I sometimes wonder at the courage it must have taken for my sick Daddy to undergo all of this, but he was fighting for a motherless family and seemed to gather strength from necessity.

And I can remember after almost fifty years, the long talks he gave

---

6   Water puppies are a colloquial term for salamanders

me—counseling, warning, encouraging and inspiring me to try for the best, and to put my mark high and try to reach it.

After a twenty, or maybe twenty-two, acre tract of the virgin, sod-covered grass had been torn loose from its network of buffalo grass roots and turned its skinny black ribbons of soil skyward, we would pack again and the old wagon would begin the homeward journey. Now we could plan something, as we would have the twenty to thirty dollars we had earned, and "Oh! How we needed it!"

Usually we had found seven or eight pairs of (cow or calf) buffalo horns that were still in a good state of preservation, and my Daddy would take them home and rasp off the loose rough outside. Then he would sandpaper them and then use emery paper and polish them into a beautiful, glossy black, which he would make into hat racks, coat racks, footstools, and gun racks. These he would take to town and sell to eastern people for five to ten dollars as souvenirs of the West. Money earned this way often saved the day for us and helped to keep the wolf from the door of the little sod house as well as furnishing the easterners some useful products of the far West. They usually brought $5-$10 each if we fixed them up with plush and brass-headed tacks.

We acquired several calves and raised the heifers for milk cows. We churned and made butter and cheese. We raised chickens and had plenty of eggs, had a nice garden and raised wheat that made a good yield, but had to be threshed by means of leading or driving horses round and round, trampling it out. Then we had to laboriously clean out the chaff and straw by hand. We raised corn and planted cow peas with it. These we kept for winter use. We girls were little by little learning the cooking and housekeeping arts and now we could plainly see that Grandmother had been right about us learning them in Missouri on the farm.

By now our Grandmother (Elizabeth Ann Doughty) was all settled on a homestead about two miles from ours. It was south of the new railroad and we soon had a beaten pathway to it. She taught my sister and me to bake nice light bread. We printed a nice, little sign, "Bread For Sale", and when the long caravan of white canvas-covered "prairie schooners" appeared coming over the top of the hill that we called "Kit Carson's Fort" because of a legend that he had once fought Indians there, we scampered for our sign, our little red or blue calico Mother Hubbards flapping in the breeze. We hastily erected it in the most conspicuous place, and waited hopefully for customers. The home-seeking westerners, tired of the cramped quarters of the wagons and tired of eating bread fried in a skillet or Dutch oven, usually climbed out and after asking all about the new railroad, the crops and the prospects of making a go of it, would buy our entire supply. Little by little we were learning to watch all the little corners to help make a living.

Often these large groups of wagons traveling together would approach our place about sundown and that meant they would camp for the night. We would make short work of supper and the dishes, and then accompanied by our father, would clean up and hasten out to the visiting wagons, and perhaps get acquainted with some new neighbors or settlers. The men would sit in scattered groups on wagon tongues, boxes or remove the spring seats from the wagon for seats while the women were stirring about and the children playing games of hide-and-seek. After a while, someone would bring out an old fiddle and tune it up, and someone else would strike into a song, then another and another. Some of the old songs were, "Little Old Sod Shanty on the Plains," "Roosters Grow Tall in Kansas,"[7] "The Elevated Railway,"[8] "Never Take the Horseshoe From The Door" and "The Cat That Came Back." The red ashes from the campfires began to grow to a whitish gray and the chill from the mountains to the west would begin creeping in. The little ones nestled closer and closer to their mothers. After

---

[7]   This possibly refers to a folksong of the time called "In Kansas" (circa 1840). One version contains the lines: "Oh, the girls they do grow tall in Kansas" and "The roosters they lay eggs in Kansas"

[8]   This song probably refers to the folksong "Riding on the Elevated Railroad" written in 1878. (www.traditionalmusic.co.uk)

the fiddler grew tired, the men talked on and on, perhaps some boy brought out a mouth harp and played awhile and then "good nights" were said, the beds in the covered wagons made up, and soon all were making ready for the night. We were always sorry to lose our new acquaintances among the children and would sleepily follow our father to our sod house across the road from the encampment.

Nearly always the morning following the encampment, my father put over a horse trade, for usually there were some foot-sore horses that traveled badly. He would get a few dollars to boot, and trade them a fresh horse that was not foot sore, and the few dollars, thus obtained, bought more flour for us to make more bread and thus keep our larder supplied. "Where there's a will, there's a way," I've found to certainly be true, as true now in 1935 as it was in 1886, but as the wagons moved away the next morning, carrying with them all our newly found playmates, life seemed lonely, listless and dull for several days. But healthy, vigorous youth and childhood will always find something to fill in the lonely hours no matter where located, and as I watched the newcomers unloading the big square pine boxes containing their treasures, my hopes turned to the possibility of borrowing some books to read. I had read every book I could borrow in the neighborhood and the possibility of new stories was a welcome daydream. I had read "The Scottish Chiefs" and in the same box was "Lorna Doone" and a "History of England" and some books on the history of the Reformation, all of which I had labored through, and in a way enjoyed. The "Scottish Chiefs" made me very sad and I wept and cried over Sir William Wallace and his tribulations and would throw the book on top of an exceedingly high cupboard when the story got too tragical and declare I never would read it any more, then finally fish it out again and read some more. I was now about twelve years-old and when all else failed, would borrow a botany or geography book and pore over it on long cold winter nights with a hand-made grease light, which was string twisted together and laid about in a pie pan of melted lard, one end raised up and lighted to form a light. The idea that I was born to be a teacher was creeping in, as so many of my relatives had followed this work, and I felt I must hurry and prepare myself with this in mind. I began inquiring of everybody the way to go about it. My Aunt Julia Doughty had come from Missouri and taught a term of school which I attended at the old Crystal Springs School. I began memorizing the reviews at the end of the chapters in history, geography and grammar. I learned the answers to thousands of map questions, learned by heart most all the poems in my readers, borrowed a pamphlet on the school laws of Colorado and studied it far into the night, with the grease lamp sputtering a little light in the darkness of the big bedroom of the sod house. My father would call me and demand I blow it out and immediately get to sleep. I'd agree and then read on until I awoke to find it morning and my father had put out the grease light and moved it away from its perch on the pine box by my bedside, and I had to hurry and get up to help get breakfast.

About this time, my sister who was four years older than I, had received a certificate to teach. She was about sixteen and I was a little past twelve. About that time, my Aunt Julia was preparing to take an examination given at Flagler in the school house. I pleaded and begged to try too, but they only laughed at me. Finally they said I could go along and see if they would permit me to just take a test for practice. Upon arriving, she explained what I wanted to the examiner and he smilingly gave consent. I wrote the whole examination and passed in a few subjects. I was disappointed but more determined than ever, so renewed my studies with more zeal than ever. I burned the grease lamp, and sometimes coal oil when we happened to have it, far into the night. I burned stacks of cow chips, the only fuel available. I almost ruined my eyes and all my books were taken away to my grandmother's house, but I still had "Scottish Chiefs" on top of the cupboard and the sorrows and sufferings of Sir William and Lady Wallace caused me to shed tears of grief, much as the movie fans do today over the hero and heroine's sufferings. My sister was now away teaching. My brother, Frank, was in Denver working to get a little money to help out. My father was at his mother's a great deal of the time so I was the head of the house and kept my two small brothers. On a trip home, by big brother bought "The Children of the Abbey," which I read and re-read. I also acquired a copy of Lord Tennyson's poems somewhere. They, too, were lots of help.

At the sod school house on cold, starry, wintry nights with the ground covered with snow, the people would gather in for "Literaries," spelling matches, ciphering matches and sometimes singing school. Someone who understood music, usually some teacher, would teach us how to sing "by note" and get the right pitch and then we'd sing some old songs and go home humming tunes. It all helped a lot. Once in a great while a magic lantern show would arrive and put on a program at the sod school house. They were very much enjoyed, and discussed on the walk home over the beautiful sparkling snow. The champion spellers—how they did study the spelling books and pronounce the words to each other in hopes of holding the championship. This would all seem very tame to my children and grandchildren. Now they can climb into a warm, heated, cushioned car and speed along beautiful paved highways at sixty to eighty miles per hour, and drive up to a movie theater without any physical discomfort, like frosted hands or feet of bygone years. They can witness a moving, talking picture, the news reels of the world and hear wonderful music and then step back into the high-powered heated car and are soon home again to electric lights, furnace heat or electric fan as the need may be. It is all so very easy. In fact, I believe it is too easy, as people forget to be grateful and appreciative when possessed of too many luxuries. This present generation is living in a world far more wonderful than the stories of Hans Christian Andersen. Fairy stories have been eclipsed by realities and words, like the first words sent over the telegraph wires, "What hath God wrought," cease to bring awe or gratitude to our hearts. Like spoiled children, we only clamor for more wonders, greater miracles, more ease and a faster, easier life. The things that should bring more leisure and fuller, happier lives seem only to overcrowd them.

The days were speeding by. My sister's school was out and she came home during the summer. My father's health was much better. He plowed forty or fifty acres of the buffalo grass sod and we planted crops of corn, wheat, cane, millet and a large garden. Our flock of cattle had grown to forty or more, and by trading and raising colts, we had a drove of fifty to sixty horses. Eastern people kept coming; more land was taken up, more sod houses were being built, school districts were organized, and little one-room schoolhouses began to dot the prairies. A church was built at Flagler and regular services held. It was of the Congregational denomination. Sunday Schools were becoming popular out in the country school houses.

Some of the new settlers brought some money into the country. Several nice homes were built. One I remember, especially, was the house built in Flagler by a Mr. Cornwall. A flour mill was built and did quite a business. We took our wheat there and exchanged it for flour. Windmills began to spring up over the prairie. These were used to water gardens as well as the cattle.

The day of the Texas Longhorn cattle was passing and other larger breeds replacing them. These new settlers were from the older states and brought many new, progressive ideas and tossed them into the melting pot, along with western ideas and in this way, the great new west was born—destined to become the home of many progressive people. Of course, many of them gave up, threw up their rights to the land and left, but a majority remained to be among the leading citizens and proved that courage and grit win. Several little fruit orchards were planted and watered with windmills. The one on the Lind place, east of town, became a pretty good orchard. The orchard of Jim Howell, northeast of town, flourished and was a veritable oasis in the desert. It was a wonder and comfort to all who visited it and were lucky enough to get to pick some cherries. It only needed some determined people to duplicate it on many of the homesteads that had similar advantages of springs and sloping land.

With the coming of the railroad, came doctors, lawyers, and ministers, who sometimes eked out a meager minister's salary by teaching a short term of school. I remember a Preacher Smith who did this. I attended the school at the Crystal Springs sod school house. County elections were held and officers elected. Burlingame [Burlington?] became the County Seat.

Either I have forgotten, or else I did not hear of it, but as far as I know, crimes were not frequent, there was very little theft or murder, and very few divorces. Mothers and fathers were happily busy with their children. Big dances were held in the hall above the school house on Christmas Day, New Year's Day, Election Day and St. Patrick's Day.

In the autumn, the round up and shipping of the fat cattle to Kansas City caused quite a little stir in most of the small railroad towns. The warm autumn days were disturbed by the bawling of calves out for branding and every ranch had several cow-men with good saddles and saddle horses. Even housewives, who often spent silent, lonely hours during the winter and spring, felt the happy thrill of expectancy for now some new clothing could be bought, and perhaps a few badly needed pieces of furniture or carpets, dishes, stoves, etc. could be purchased. After the cattle had at last been loaded and on the freight trains headed for Kansas City, usually accompanied by the owners, the patient, loving wives and mothers could at least let their fancies run riot and plan for lots of new things for their homes, their children and for themselves. It was a long, anxious wait until the husbands and fathers returned and brought some nice presents from the great far away city and at last they knew exactly what the cattle had brought and just what they could afford for general expenses after debts, store bills, taxes and all other obligations had been subtracted. Arrangements were made for new bulls to head the herds, feed for stock, more wire for fencing, more land, and perhaps lumber for shed roofs. Often the wives' dreams must be sadly curtailed for these necessities. The "old coat" must be worn again for perhaps the 3rd or 4th winter, sometimes their "wedding coat and fascinator," or summer things, depending on the season, must be worn on the occasions like Christmas and New Years, until the family was about half-grown.

The dry goods boxes must be used season after season for cupboards, clothes cupboards, wash stands and many other things and it was a grand day when the time finally came for some new store cupboards, dressers, chairs or stoves, but all in all, they were a contented, industrious, serious people. These history makers of the west, having once "set their hands to the plow", did not look back but forged slowly and steadily on, preparing the way for the onward march of the, as yet unborn generations, toward the snow-capped Rockies and fertile plains and valleys awaiting in towns, cities, mines of gold, great highways, a wondrous system of schools and colleges and great daily newspapers, all as yet in the formative stage, just around the corner.

Introduction To Lester's Story

LESTER WAS THE eldest of seven children born to Adda and Henry Brookhart. Born in January of 1900, his life included a front-row seat to some of the most significant events in our modern history. He tells the story of his life—and that of his family—amid the backdrop of WWI, the Spanish Flu of 1918, WWII, the Great Depression, and the great plains Dust Bowl. In less ornate language than his mother, Lester lays out his story which includes precious breadcrumbs that "fill out" the family history. Lester was industrious, having worked many kinds of jobs, including teaching school like his mother, before settling in as an agent for the Internal Revenue Service.

Lester Raymond Brookhart— An Autobiography

MY FATHER WAS Henry Clifford Brookhart, who was born in Palmyra, Iowa. He lived in this town until he was twenty-one years of age. He had heard of California and planned to go there to seek his fortune. Before final arrangements had been made he heard that some new land was being opened up for homesteading in Oklahoma Indian Territory, and was known as the Cherokee Strip. The land was in north central Oklahoma. He, and his two brothers, Newton Samuel Brookhart, and William Brookhart, his mother Catharine Minerva Brookhart, and his cousin, Charles Owens, decided to take land in this new territory. In September of 1893 they lined up together with thousands of others on the Kansas State line. At the sound of a canon, as a signal, they started out to find a new home.

My father rode a horse known as Fred. His mother and brother William (who was not 21 years of age and therefore could not take land) rode in a covered wagon in which their belongings were packed. My father found some desirable land about six miles south of what is now the town of Tonkawa, Oklahoma. The land consisted of 160 acres of rich farming land drained by a small creek known as Birds Nest Creek.

After "staking out" or putting flags on the boundaries to indicate the land was taken, he had to go to the town of Perry in what is now

Noble County to register the land in his name. While in the land office he began talking to a stranger, and found that the stranger was rather disgusted with the land he planned to claim and had decided to go back to his home. He gave the description of the land to my father's mother and she proceeded to file on the land. Strangely enough, she found that this land was adjoining the land my father had filed on and my father's cousin, Charles Owens, filed on some land that joined my father's land on the other side, so they all had land and were located very close together. The brother, Newton, went on, some 30 miles father south and filed on some land near a place that later became the town of Morrison, Oklahoma.

My father fenced his farm, built a house, barn, and other necessary buildings, dug a well, planted fruit trees, plowed up the natural vegetation, and planted crops. He also helped his mother do the same to her land across the road. The neighbors improved their farms and the community soon became an industrious and productive farming area.

My mother, Adda Blanche Brookhart, had lived in Colorado. At the age of 15 she obtained a teacher's certificate and taught school in the vicinity of Flagler, Colorado.

During her summer vacation, she visited her father, Benjamin Doughty, who had a department store in Arkansas City, Kansas, a short distance from the Oklahoma Territory line. Someone told her that there was a school across the line in Oklahoma Territory that wanted a teacher. She rented a horse and buggy and drove down to the school, applied for the job and was promptly hired. The school happened to be about two miles from the land owned by my father and was known as the Eagle's Nest School. During the course of the term of school, Father and Mother became acquainted, fell in love, and on April 23, 1899 were married. They met in the town of Newkirk, near the border and my mother's father helped officiate.

They proceeded to build a larger house and lived on the farm. One stormy night on the 27th of January, 1900, I was born. A country doctor known as Dr. Witter attended the event. The entire cost of my layette and doctor's fee amounted to $15.00. This is quite a contrast to today's charges.

I was a normal baby with an unusually large amount of black hair. A neighbor lady came to visit my mother and remarked that "all of Esau's tribe had not died yet." This was a reference to a Biblical character who was noted for his abundance of hair. My mother was a little offended by this remark.

On March 31, 1901, my sister Lila was born. She, too, was a healthy baby and I soon had a companion to play with.

As a baby I was healthy and grew rapidly as most babies do, until one day some neighbors paid my mother a visit. This was when I was about two years old. The neighbor's children who came along were coughing. My mother asked the mother what the reason for the cough was and was told that it, "was only a case of whooping cough."

At this point, it was too late to prevent contagion, and in due time I contracted the disease. It greatly weakened me and I was very sick. Soon I showed a rickety condition with considerable loss of weight. In those days the use of vitamin D and sunlight in the treatment of a vitamin D deficiency were unknown. However, Dr. Witter recommended Scott's Emulsion[9] which is rich in Vitamin D and I slowly began to improve.

My mother had obtained some land in Colorado under the homestead law which she wanted to improve and sell. She also thought that the Colorado climate would be good for my health. So, the farm was rented and we moved to Colorado in the spring of 1902.

The Colorado land had no house on it and we stayed with relatives while a house was being built. My earliest recollection was about this time. It was summer and the frogs were croaking one evening when I volunteered to accompany my Aunt Myrtle to the well to get some

---

9   Scott's Emulsion, a cod liver oil preparation, is still available today.

water, in order to protect her from the frogs.

Soon our house was completed. It was constructed of sod squares with walls about two feet thick and a sod roof. It proved to be warm and comfortable we lived there several years. The home was on the Republican River near a spring and about three miles southeast of the town of Flagler, Colorado. It was in this general area where my mother had taught school before her move to Oklahoma.

It was while living here that my sister, Viola Blanche was born and later, my brother Clifford Owens, making four children in our family.

My earliest childhood days were spent here roaming along the banks of the Republican River. Our home was about one-half mile from the Rock Island Railroad and I often watched the trains with childish wonderment. On two occasions there were wrecks and I watched the wrecking crew pick up the cars and put them on the tracks.

My great grandmother, Elizabeth Christian Doughty lived near us and I would often go to visit her. She would always serve me with some cookies and a glass of milk. She lived there for many years and died at the age of 93 years.

One day while watching the trains, I found what seemed to me to be a very odd looking object. I put it in my pocket for further examination at home. At home I secured a hammer and a large piece of iron, put the object on it, and was getting ready to strike it with the hammer, when my father intervened, took the object away from me and threw it into a pond. It was a dynamite cap, used to signal the engineer to slow or stop the train. I was very disappointed, but it only shows that children do not always appreciate the protection that parents give them. If I had struck the object, I might have been killed or blinded for life.

At another time, when I was about four years old our family went to a Fourth of July celebration at a nearby town called Siebert. I and several older boys were shooting fire crackers. Since the middle of the street was a nice open space, that is where we went. A wild west show of bucking broncos was scheduled as part of the celebration and, while we were absorbed in the firecrackers, a herd of wild horses came running down the street. The older boys saw the horses and ran. Before I realized it, the horses were upon me. I crouched down and they all went around me. I wore a white shirt which caused the horse to shy and miss me altogether. My mother was in a panic for she was sure that I had been killed, but I had not a scratch.

When I was almost six years of age, my parents decided to sell the Colorado land and move back to the Oklahoma farm. Arrangements were soon made and my brothers and sisters and I were very excited about getting to ride the trains that we had so often seen near our home. It took about 24 hours to travel the 400 miles to our farm in Oklahoma. Our father had rented a box car or "immigrant car"[sic] from the railroad and we arrived a few days later with our livestock, farm tools and household goods. We were soon located on the farm and it was time to enroll in the local one-room school. This school was located about three-quarters of a mile from our home and was known as the "Frog Holler School" because it was located in a low area near a creek inhabited by many frogs. The name was later changed to the Hope School. There were about 25 children enrolled in the school in all eight grades and under one teacher. Those in the lower grades would listen to the older grades recite and thus got a double exposure to the textbook material. During the winter months, we would skate and build the customary snow men. The sunflower grew rather luxuriously in the summer to a height of about eight feet. In the fall we used the stalks to build teepees and small play houses by weaving the stalks together.

On July 21st, 1906, a new baby brother was born, my brother, Kenneth. He was a very happy and healthy baby. This made five children in our family. My mother's sister, Aunt Myrtle Doughty stayed with us for a while and helped to care for the children.

One April afternoon in 1912 the school that we attended was

visited by a heavy rain and hail storm. After the storm was over about four o'clock in the afternoon, we were making preparations to go home when we noticed a long circular cloud extending from the clouds above to the ground. This was about two miles to the southwest of where we were. The twisting cloud, known as a tornado, was coming directly toward us. When it reached a distance of about one-half mile of the school and was headed directly toward the school, the teacher gathered the group together and decided that we would attempt to run away from the tornado's path. This we did and were successful, but finally it veered away from the school house and went over a hill, destroying the home of one of the students. This was quite common in this area and many a night our parents would take us to a storm cellar (underground) which was built as protection against these storms. Tornados occurred at other times and we were often able to observe their destructive effects.

During the summer vacations we would explore the banks of the Birds Nest Creek which flowed through the farm. There were catfish, perch, and buffalo fish, turtles, snakes, frogs, crawdads (crawfish), clams, birds of many kinds, rabbits, skunks, opossums, and many other kinds of animal life. The horse my father had ridden at the opening of the Cherokee Strip was named Fred and we children thought much of him. He was gentle and we rode him often. It was a very happy life and we were all a happy healthy group.

One evening about dusk, my sister, Lila, and I noticed a funny star with a fuzzy tail on it. Our father explained that it was a comet and it proved to be the forerunner of Halley's Comet which was to appear several months later. When Halley's Comet appeared in the spring of 1910, it was at first barely visible, but as it approached it seemed to become larger. We were told that the earth was to pass through the tail of the comet, which it did. This aroused much discussion as to the possible dire consequences. Some people thought that this would be the end of the world. Some school children cried at the prospect of having the comet destroy the world. All sorts of dire calamities were predicted. About two o'clock one morning our mother aroused us children from our sleep and told us to come and look at the comet. There it was emblazoned across the eastern sky with the head pointed toward the south. It was a spectacular sight, a sight I shall never forget. It covered most of the eastern sky and the tail was as bright as the other stars in the heavens. My mother had a difficult time getting me to go back to bed. I wanted to watch it until morning. It is scheduled to appear again about the year 1986 and will probably be just as spectacular then. As you read this, resolve not to miss it if you are alive then![10]

One afternoon my two sisters, Lila and Viola were sent to the mailbox about a half mile away to get the mail. After a considerable time had elapsed and they did not return, my father went to see what was wrong. He was unable to find them or any trace of them. We began telephoning our neighbors to see if any of them had seen the girls but with no results. Finally we became alarmed and alerted all the neighbors to help hunt for them. It was getting dark and the neighbors lighted their lanterns and started the search. Finally we contacted a lady by telephone who said she had seen the girls walking along the road near her home. My mother and I immediately got into our buggy and our father got on a horse and we started the search. After traveling about five miles to the edge of an Indian Reservation, we spotted the two girls footsore and weary. Upon seeing us they explained that they, "were trying to get home before dark" and, "There wasn't any mail in the mail box." It soon became dark and we returned home. We could see our neighbors' lanterns everywhere as they continued the search. By a prearranged signal my father shot off a shot gun three times indicating that the girls had been found. The neighbors immediately came to our house and my mother prepared coffee and hot oyster soup for all of them to help show our appreciation for their help.

---

10   Halley's Comet was visible in the spring of 1986; the next appearance will be in 2061.

We lived about two miles from a United Brethren church and every Sunday our parents would take us to church and Sunday school, where we learned Bible verses and Bible stories. Later the church became the Christian Church and we became members as long as we lived in Oklahoma. The church was by a cemetery known as the Prairie View Cemetery and is located about five or six miles south and a little east of Tonkawa. My grandmother Catharine Owens Brookhart is buried there. My grandmother, at that time, lived in the town of Tonkawa about six miles from us and I often visited her. One summer about 1910 when she was not well I stayed most of the summer with her, helping her with the yard and household chores and running errands for her. She often told me stories of her childhood days in Pennsylvania and taught me the principles of thrift.

One day a man stopped at our home and explained that he wanted to lease our land and drill for oil. It was hard to believe that there should be oil under the land and my father, with little persuasion, signed a lease. He should have waited, for others received a considerable bonus for signing the lease and sold part of the royalties for considerable amounts. The oil company began drilling in the vicinity but with no important results. Later the story was different.

My mother's health seemed to be failing. Our well water was very hard and contained considerable amounts of gypsum. Her doctor thought that her liver was causing her trouble and blamed it on the hard water. He advised her to move to where the water was softer. Colorado had a reputation of being a very healthful climate. Father and she decided to rent the farm and move to Colorado. They conducted a sale in December, 1912 and sold most of the cattle, farm machinery, and household goods, and rented the farm. Father again rented an emigrant railroad car and loaded the remaining livestock aboard, consisting of a pony, two cows, two horses, and two dogs. Mother and we children traveled by railroad coach to Colorado. We arrived December 12, 1912 and stayed with Mother's sister, Mollie

Verhoeff at McClave, Colorado until our father arrived. We rented a house in Las Animas, Colorado and immediately all of us children were enrolled in school. We lived in Las Animas about a year when my parents bought a thirty-acre parcel of land about one-half mile west of Las Animas. We settled down and this place became our home. We children attended the Columbian School, a red brick, two-story grade school in Las Animas[11]. Later we attended the Bent County High School there. The thirty acre plot later became the Brookhart Nursery which furnished flowers, shrubs, and trees for Las Animas. Most of the shade trees in Las Animas today came from the nursery.

The family joined the Christian Church and became active in church activities. My father became a member of the Odd Fellows Lodge and took an active part. My mother always taught a Sunday school class and was in the Women's Christian Temperance Union. She would often give lectures on temperance. There were saloons in Las Animas in these days of the old type and the number of drunks on the streets caused a problem. The church discouraged dancing and card playing, but there were many skating parties, picnics, and social parties in the public schools, the church and the home, so there was plenty of social life.

While in high school my parents bought me a violin and I started taking violin lessons. My sister, Lila, was already an accomplished pianist. My music teacher was a Mr. Peters, a German navy man who had been interned in America during the European war. He was a very good teacher, having studied in a conservatory in Germany. However, when the United States went to war with Germany in 1917, Mr. Peters was taken as a prisoner of war and my violin lessons had to stop. I regretted this as I like the violin very much. I continued to play in a Sunday school orchestra until I left Las Animas to go to college.

---

11   The Columbian School was constructed in 1887, but replaced by the Columbian Elementary School built in 1916. The original Columbian School, despite efforts to preserve it, was demolished in 2006. (Coloradopreservation.org)

My sister, Lila, had been "going steady" with one of her classmates in high school, John Sleeth. When the war started he knew it would be a matter of time until he would be drafted for military service. So, he enlisted in the navy and was sent to the Great Lakes Training Camp. Before he enlisted, he and Lila were married in a quiet wedding in our home. He was a postman in Las Animas and returned to this job after the end of the war.

We still owned the farm in Oklahoma and rumors persisted that there was an oil boom there. My father received a good offer for the farm and he sold it, not knowing what the future held in oil development. One of our neighbors, Sam McKee, who lived one mile east of the farm had leased his land to the oil company. Sam was a very hard worker and had a big family. One day when he and his sons were working in the field he looked up and saw an incredible sight. Oil was shooting over the over the top of the oil derrick. He said to his sons, "Drive the team in boys, we won't have to work any more." Later Mr. McKee visited my family in Colorado. We asked about the oil strike and how much he had made. He replied that he did not know for sure but it was somewhere between seven and eight million and that the last he knew his income was about $85,000 per month.

No well was ever drilled on my father's Oklahoma farm but if he had kept the land he would have been able to sell oil royalties for at least $50,000 which was quite a fortune in those days. Some of his old neighbors were more fortunate and were able to realize considerable sums for their oil royalties.

We still had the pony which we had brought from Oklahoma and we children like to ride it. A friend of mine, Maynard Shipley, a nephew of the Indian scout, Kit Carson, also had a pony and we went many places together. He had a brother who had a large cattle ranch about twenty miles south of Las Animas. I would often go with him for a visit to this ranch for a week or so and watch the rounding up and branding of cattle. Once we rode to La Junta, Colorado, about twenty miles away to see the Sells-Floto Circus. Buffalo Bill Cody and Annie Oakley, the expert rifle shot, were with the circus. Buffalo Bill was on a white horse and rode around the arena in the tent to the enthusiastic applause of the crowd. My friend and I enjoyed the trip very much and arrived home late that night after the forty mile ride.

In 1917 my father bought his first automobile. It was a Willys-Knight, manufactured by the Willys-Overland Company of Toledo, OH. Instead of the usual poppet valves in the engine, the valves consisted of two sleeves, fitted between the piston and the cylinder and operated by short connecting rods connected to the cam shaft. The oil pump consisted of a piston and cylinder. Water would often condense in the cylinder and freeze, so that when the engine was started the connecting rod would break. The car was poorly designed by modern standards, so that after it had gone 15,000 miles, the expense of constant repairs made it unprofitable to operate. My father purchased a model T Ford which proved much more practical and economical to operate. He continued to drive the Ford until about 1929 when he purchased a Model A Ford.

During the summer months, my brothers, other boys in the neighborhood, and I would go to Kansas for the wheat harvest. The pay was four or five dollars a day which was good wages then. The work consisted of loading the wheat onto "barges" or wagons where it was hauled to the definite spot to be stacked. Later the threshing machine would come and thresh the grain. The harvest lasted about four weeks and we would often return with about $100 or more. Later the method of harvesting was changed to the "combine" where the grain was threshed as it was cut in the field. This ended the demand for extra help in the Kansas wheat harvest.

April 1917 found the United States at war with Germany. My sister Lila's husband, John Sleeth, enlisted and went to the Navy training camp. Lila took a job in the local telegraph office, delivering telegrams. I took over John's postal route in Las Animas temporarily. There was considerable patriotic spirit with marching bands, sales of war bonds, and other patriotic activities. The draft was soon adopted as a means of increasing the armed to war strength. I was not old enough for the first draft but late in the summer of 1918 I registered for the second draft. I felt that the war was wrong but since my country was in trouble, I should enlist and do my part. I did not wait for the draft but enlisted in the Student Army Training Corp at Colorado College at Colorado Springs. We were to take two or three college courses a day and spend most of the rest of each day with army drill. The purpose was to make army officers of the enlistees.

The "Spanish Influenza" had hit Europe and was claiming many lives. Soon it was in the United States. It hit Army camps especially hard and many were dying.

In camp I became homesick and one Friday in October I asked my captain for a weekend furlough, which was granted. I boarded a train for my home which was about 120 miles away, intending to return the following Sunday afternoon. I awoke Sunday morning with a temperature of 103°F. I had the "flu" and was not to return to camp for five weeks. My parents hired a special nurse and I had the best of care. Dr. Hagerman of Las Animas was my doctor. It was the first case of the disease in Las Animas and no one knew what to do for it. All theatres, churches, schools, and public meetings were closed to avoid spreading the disease, but many died anyway. Some of my friends in Las Animas inquired of Dr. Hagerman as to my progress. He told them that I could not live. Later my friends were surprised to see me on the streets and told me that they had heard that I had died, a slight exaggeration.

I received my doctor's consent to return to camp on November 11, 1918. On that morning the whistles began to blow, the bells to ring, and people everywhere began to celebrate. The war was over! However my orders were to return to camp, so I did. It was not long after that, that we were sent home. I was given a "temporary" discharge and told that the final discharge would follow. However, the army records were boxed and shipped to Washington, D.C. and my record could not be located. It was about twenty years later that I received my honorable discharge after considerable correspondence with the Department of the Army.

By January of 1919 the schools reopened and I completed my high school education that had been interrupted by the war. The next day after graduation I took a United States Civil Service examination for the position of rural mail carrier for the post office. Three other men and I took the examination and I received the appointment. The route was fifty miles long and started from the town of Caddoa, Colorado. Caddoa was twenty miles east of Las Animas, Colorado. I purchased a Model T Ford and reported for duty. Later the town was moved when the Martin Damn was built on the Arkansas River and the site of the old town is now under water. I carried the mail until late in the summer of 1920. By this time I had saved enough money so that I could enter college, so I resigned my job and went to Phillips University at Enid, Oklahoma. I was persuaded to go to this college by friends in the Christian Church in Las Animas, who thought that this was the only college where I would not receive an education contrary to the teachings of the Christian Church. They thought that I should prepare myself for the ministry. After one year here I decided that it was not the college for me and decided to enter Colorado College the next fall, where I had attended as part of the Student Army Training Corp program in World War I.

I went home to Las Animas during the summer months in hopes of finding a summer job. On June 2, 1921, the Arkansas River got out of its banks after a hard rain storm and flooded Las Animas and the surrounding area. The river flooded my parents' nursery causing severe damage to the nursery stock and caused a great financial loss. I worked that summer sorting pickles for Libby McNeil and Libby Co. at 40¢ per hour. This helped me to enter college that fall at Colorado College, where I completed another year of college work. During the year I fired furnaces and worked in a restaurant to supplement the money I had saved for college.

In the spring of 1922 I took a teacher's examination at Colorado Springs but without any serious intention of entering the teaching profession. I passed the examination with better grades than I had anticipated and later that spring a school board member of a small consolidated school known as the Ellicott School, contacted me and asked if I would accept a job teaching in the high school. Ellicott is located about twenty miles east of Colorado Springs. Since my savings were about exhausted, I accepted. After signing the contract I went to Las Animas to find a job for the summer. One job that I had during the summer was that of assistant pipe fitter for the Santa Fe Railroad at La Junta, Colorado. There were many pipes on the steam locomotives, some for steam, some for water, and some for compressed air. My job was to help replace or repair pipes and valves as needed. The job was noisy and hot but it paid well and helped me to buy some clothes for my new job.

In September, I reported for my teaching job. I was to teach Physics, Algebra, Spanish, English, and manual training. I also coached the basketball and track teams. I received $900 for the year (of nine months) and was furnished living quarters in the basement of the school. I had to study hard to keep ahead of my classes but it kept me busy during the long winter evenings. It was my first attempt at teaching and the quality of the instruction could have improved, however, my basketball team took second place among the consolidated schools of the county and my track team won several first places. I saved a good part of the $900 for college expenses for the next year.

During the summer of 1923, I first took a job selling newspapers, cigars, candy, etc. For Fred Harvey on the Santa Fe railroad line between Denver and Dodge City, Kansas. It involved irregular hours, sleeping on the train and not much net income. I had previously applied for a job as room clerk for Longs Peak Inn in the Rocky Mountain

National Park in Colorado and when the job was offered me I accepted and worked for the rest of the summer there. Most of the employees were college students and the summer proved to be very pleasant. It was while here that I started to learn how to dance. It had been taboo in my hometown, Las Animas.

Longs Peak Inn had been built by a man by the name of Enos Mills. He had written about fifteen books about the Rocky Mountains and wildlife there. He had many author friends who would come to the Inn and many of them would spend the summer there. Edna Ferber stayed at the Inn most of the summer and I had many conversations with her. As I remember, she was writing her book, *So Big*, at the time. She was a very interesting person and had a profound understanding of human nature.

I went back to Colorado College in the fall of 1923 and completed another year of college work. I also continued to work at odd jobs to supplement my savings. I took care of children, read to sick people, mowed lawns, worked in a restaurant, waited tables, and did numerous other jobs. I continued to learn to dance, taking advantage of a class offered by the college in the evenings. One of the girls' gym classes served as instructors.

I had not, at this time, made up my mind just what work or profession I would choose for my life work. My chief interest in the college courses I had completed was in economics, sociology, history, business, and the life sciences.

My room-mate, Clay Freudenberger, was preparing for a medical career in the footsteps of his father and wanted me to study medicine. I knew how expensive the medical preparation would be and how limited my finances were so did not consider the choice very seriously. In high school I had written up high school events for the local newspaper and thought that I might follow journalism as a career. One day I expressed this desire to one of my college professors. He suggested that I read *The Brass Check* by Upton Sinclair which I did. It had a rather dim view of journalism as a career. The reading of this book was instrumental in my decision not to choose journalism for my life work. This decision may or may not have been wise. Many years later I met Upton Sinclair and during my conversation with him, told him of my decision based on his book. He said that if he had helped me in any way, he was glad. He then went briefly into his own life, how he worked and wrote. He seemed very satisfied that he had chosen writing as a life work.

I had taught a year and had enjoyed it. It offered the opportunity of alternating teaching with a year in college, thus helping with my financial problems. My boyhood friend, Harry Harmsworth, was planning to attend Colorado State Teachers College at Greeley, Colorado. This is now Colorado State College. I decided that if I should continue to teach, I should prepare myself in a teacher's college.

During the summer of 1924 I secured a job at the YMCA Camp near Estes Park Village in the Rocky Mountain National Park, as room clerk. The camp had many summer camp groups and conventions with as many as 700 guests at a time. However, I found time to climb Longs Peak which was near. The peak was over 14,000 feet in height and commanded a glorious view from the top at sunrise. As various groups came along who wanted a guide, I would volunteer, climb all night, return to camp the next day by noon, and proceed to work until closing time at 10:00 p.m. The loss of sleep didn't bother me as I always found time to make up the loss.

In the fall of 1924 I enrolled at Colorado Teachers College at Greeley and took courses in education and the social sciences. I found that expenses were much less here. There was no tuition as there was at Colorado College, a private college. Board and room were less too. I enjoyed the term here and found the work interesting.

When summer came I secured employment at Grand Lake Lodge. The Lodge was located near the town of Grand Lake and was on a cliff about 500 feet above the lake. There was a cabaret dance hall on the lake and I would often climb down the cliff for an evening's entertainment. Victor Jory, an actor from Denver who later became famous as a movie actor was often there and I would often trade dances with him. There were many other college students who worked at the lake. A group would often arrange a cook-out or wiener roast at the edge of the lake. Sometimes we would get in a boat and serenade people who had cabins around the lake. I had a mandolin and would lead the group in singing. Sometimes we were invited into the cabins for a treat.

In the fall of 1925 I found that my finances were again at a low ebb and I decided that it would be necessary to teach the following year. Through a teacher's agency in Denver, I secured a job as principal of a grade school in Magdalena, New Mexico. When the summer ended at Grand Lake, I went home for a short visit at Las Animas and then boarded a train for New Mexico. I was a complete stranger in Magdalena since I had been hired through written recommendations sent to the school board.

This was during the prohibition days and there were many stills and bootleggers in Magdalena. When I got off the train, many of the local dealers in bootleg liquor thought that I was a revenue agent looking for contraband liquor. I later found out that not a drop of liquor was obtainable in Magdalena for several days until the bootleggers found out who I was.

The town was a mining town nestled in the mountains west of Socorro, New Mexico. About two-thirds of the population were of Spanish descent and many were *mestizo* or a mixture of Spanish and Indian. There was a very rough element in the town. Also there were people of education and refinement. The school of which I was principal had eight teachers, three of whom were Spanish. My janitor could not understand a word of English. I had studied Spanish in college and this helped, although sometimes I had to get one of the Spanish teachers to interpret. I soon learned more Spanish by conversations that I had ever learned from a book.

About one-half of the teachers were from out-of-state. We formed a club and played cards and took trips into the surrounding country to provide entertainment. There were frequent public dances which we attended. The local orchestra consisted of a saxophone, violin, piano, and drums. The manager of the orchestra convinced me that I should get a banjo and learn to play chords and thereby give more rhythm to the music. This I did and after several months of practice was playing with them. We teachers frequently journeyed to Socorro, New Mexico to dances put on by the State School of Mines.

I taught part of the eighth grade classes and did the usual duties around a grade school. The building was a fairly new building. The bell for signaling the beginning of school and the end of the noon lunch hour was on the old building about a block away. It was necessary for the janitor to walk this distance to ring the bell. I asked the school board to have the bell moved. They agreed but kept postponing the job. New Mexico is truly a "Land of Mañana." I requested permission to move the bell myself with the help of the janitor and the permission was granted. We secured a long rope and a strong ladder, unbolted the bell, carried it to the new building, put it in position and had it ringing within two hours. This made it far easier to ring the bell and on time!

We heard a rumor that the school district might not be able to pay us for the full year because of a shortage of funds. The teachers agreed that the first time we were not paid we would all quit teaching immediately. The school board did not want this to happen, so the money for the balance of the year was borrowed and the school continued. I had been sending money to my brother Clifford who was attending the University of Colorado at Boulder where he was studying electrical engineering.

As soon as my school term was completed I went to Colorado State Teachers College and attended summer school.

During the summer my brother, Clifford, was working for the Otis

Elevator Company installing an elevator in the Continental Oil Building. He had planned to discontinue work on August 21st. and take a short vacation before resuming his studies at the University. He went to work at eight o'clock and at about nine o'clock while on the tenth floor, the scaffolding broke beneath him and he fell to his death.

This was a terrible blow to the entire family but especially to my mother who had driven her model T Ford to Denver to take him home that afternoon. The shock seriously undermined my mother's health and I don't believe that she ever recovered.

The funeral was held in Las Animas and he was buried in the Las Animas Cemetery, south of town. At the time of his death, he was engaged to marry a very sweet girl whom he had met at college. This was a terrible blow to her also.

I returned to college in September of 1926 and completed my work toward the A B Degree[12], graduating in June of 1927, Because of my changing colleges and the extra time it took to complete the necessary education courses, it took longer to get the AB Degree than it would have, otherwise. This year my college was very fruitful. I had previously represented my college in debates with other colleges and became a member of the national honorary forensic fraternity, Pi Kappa Delta. I also acted in college plays and became a member of the honorary dramatic fraternity, Alpha Psi Omega. My social fraternity, Phi Delta Pi, provided a very satisfactory social life.

After graduation I went to Grand Lake Lodge and worked for the summer at the job that I had held before, that of commissary manager. The work consisted of ordering, receiving, unpacking, storing, and reissuing supplies for the hotel. The Rocky Mountain Teachers Agency were engaged to look for a teaching job for me. One day I received a telephone call requesting that I meet the superintendent of schools for Windsor, Colorado, in Denver for an interview. I got permission to

---

12   AB is the abbreviation for the Latin term *artium baccalaureus*. The AB is equivalent to the modern BA degree which stands for Bachelor of Arts.

make the trip and boarded a train for Denver. I met with the Windsor superintendent as planned and after an interview of about thirty minutes, I was hired for the job as principal of the junior high school. After finishing the summer job at Grand Lake, I went to Windsor and reported for work.

Windsor had a population of about three thousand and collected students from the surrounding country and bussed them to the grade school, junior high school, and high school. There were twelve teachers in my junior high school. The superintendent was a very capable and efficient man and gave me a lot of help. I set out to learn the problems of a principal.

There was a colony of Russians who had settled near Windsor. They were mostly farmers and were engaged in raising sugar beets. The beets were harvested in the fall and all the Russian children were kept out of the school to help harvest the beets. Provision was made for these students to attend summer school and it was my job to manage the summer school. I then took my vacation during the beet harvest.

I spent two years as principal of the junior high school at Windsor and liked the work. There were problems but none that couldn't be solved by a little effort. I had a fine superintendent and there were many nice people in the town. I often attended fraternity dances in Greeley and frequently dated college girls so that the same college atmosphere prevailed as when I was in college.

There was one objection, the pay was small in comparison to salaries paid by the industry. My brother, Kenneth, lived in Denver and was selling Ford cars, making from $400 to $500 per month, while I was making only $150 per month. I had taken quite a few business courses and wanted to get into business. I was offered a contract for the third year in Windsor, but I did not accept. Instead, I went to Denver and took some more business courses. My brother, Kenneth, had studied business at Denver University and asked me to room at his fraternity house, Kappa Sigma, on the Denver University campus, while taking some business courses.

In January 1930, the Rocky Mountain Teachers Agency in Denver got in touch with me and asked if I would accept a post in Wyoming. My first impulse was to refuse but my finances were getting low and in October, 1929 the stock market had crashed. Jobs were getting scarce. I finally agreed to take the job for the remainder of the school term and left for Casper, Wyoming, where I was to teach business courses in the Natrona County High School, a school with an enrollment of about 1300 students. When the term ended in June, I was offered a contract for the following year. I was glad to accept for by this time the financial condition of the country was getting worse. Many teachers as well as other professional people were out of work. I decided to stay until conditions improved, which was fortunate. I remained at Natrona County High School until 1937.

One evening in October 1930 I received a telephone call from Las Animas, Colorado. My brother Willard had been injured by a shot gun while hunting and was not expected to live. He and my other brother Adrian[13] had gone duck hunting. Willard had made the mistake of taking the gun out of the car muzzle end first. The trigger caught and caused the gun to fire, tearing a piece of flesh from his right thigh. A tourniquet was placed on his leg and he was rushed to the hospital. He had received a flesh burn and the dreaded gas bacillus that resulted, caused his death.

I left Casper, Wyoming about 8:00 p.m. for the drive to Las Animas, a distance of about 450 miles. I soon ran into a heavy rain storm. The state had been grading the roads and before I knew it, I was hopelessly bogged down in mud near the town of Chugwater, Wyoming. I worked until about four o'clock that night trying to get out of the mud without success. I then walked back about a mile to Chugwater and slept sitting in the waiting room of a small hotel until dawn. At eight o'clock

13   Harry (Adrian) was Adda's sixth child, and Willard was Adda's seventh and last child.

that morning I was able to get the state highway department to pull the car out of the mud and I continued on my way. I arrived that evening about dark at home and found that my brother had died earlier that day which was October 4th.

This was a severe blow to all the family, especially my mother. We had lost my brother, Clifford, only a few years before. Willard was a freshman in high school and president of his class. He was an outstanding student, interested in public speaking, and dramatics. He had ben very kind and helpful to his mother and father and gave them lots of help around the home. I did not like to leave my parents with their sorrow but I had to go back to my job in Wyoming.

While in Greeley, Colorado during the summer of 1931, I renewed my acquaintance with Elsie Burton, whom I had known in college. She was teaching in Hudson, Colorado, a small town east of Greeley. I started making trips to Colorado in my Model A ford a distance of about 270 miles each way. By Christmas we were engaged to be married and were married on May 21, 1932, three weeks before my school was out for the summer. Elsie came to Casper for the three weeks. When school was out we packed up and headed to California where I enrolled in the graduate school at the University of Southern California. I decided that if I were going to be a teacher, I should get a master's degree. I planned to spend the summers in California until I had attained that degree.

On March 9, 1933 my son Willard was born in Casper. He was a healthy and happy baby and we would all make the trip to California. Willard like the travel and we often took him to the beach to play in the sand.

The years spent in Casper were happy years. Elsie was socially minded and we acquired many friends. In the winter time I would often tramp through the snow hunting rabbits and during the warmer months would go trout fishing. During the long winter evening we would play bridge or dance at the Isaac Walton club house. We often camped in some of the Wyoming scenic spots.

The Great Depression was getting worse and I was thankful that I had a job. Then the school board started cutting salaries. California had some good school systems and were paying much better salaries to teachers than Wyoming. Naturally our thoughts turned to eventually going to California to live.

During the spring of 1934 Elsie's mother who lived near Fort Morgan, Colorado, found that she had cancer. She made many trips to Denver for x-ray treatment. She had some cancer specialists treat her, but to no avail, she kept becoming weaker and weaker. Elsie felt that she should go to take care of her, which we planned to do. One of our neighbors took care of Willard who was about a year old. Elsie was in Colorado several months until her mother died.

At Christmas time 1935 we went by car to visit our parents and relatives in Colorado. We visited her father and then went to my parents' home at Las Animas. We were there several days and my parents were able to see Willard, whom they had seen only briefly before as a baby. We had to get back to Casper since school stared soon after New Year's Day. We arrived in Casper on New Year's Eve. Soon after midnight we had a telephone call informing us that my father had died. We started in the morning on a return trip to Las Animas, a distance of 450 miles. My father had died rather suddenly of a stroke. This put an additional strain on my mother who was not well. My brother, Adrian, who had been attending Colorado University stayed with my mother and helped manage the nursery. It was the third tragedy to strike our family in ten years.

During the summer of 1936 Elsie and Willard stayed with her father who had been living alone near Fort Morgan, Colorado and I went to California alone to investigate the possibility of getting a job there. There seemed to be considerable prejudice in California against the hiring of out-of-state teachers. During the Depression all states felt that they should hire local teachers first. I explored all possibilities but was not able to find anything. However, I felt that surely I would be able to find a job in California later, so I headed my car for Colorado, picked up Elsie and Willard and went to Casper for another year.

When spring rolled around I was offered another contract which I signed. However, my faith that I could get a job in California was strong that when school was out I turned in my resignation and we packed and headed for California. This was June 1937. I worked most of the summer on my thesis and was able to complete all requirements for my master's degree.

About September 1, I received a telephone call from the California Teachers Association placement office asking if I would go to Corona, California the next morning and meet with the school board, to which I readily agreed. I met the school board and was promptly hired to teach the business subjects in their high school. We immediately rented a house in Corona and settled down for the winter. We enjoyed the mild California climate. The winter was quite a contrast to the cold Wyoming winters where the temperatures often dropped to 40°F below zero.

The Corona school system was well run with a good faculty and good superintendent. I enjoyed the year. My brother, Adrian, and his wife, Irene, visited us for a while around Christmas time. Near the end of the school term, I was offered a contract for the following year. During the previous summer, I had applied for a teaching job at Fullerton Junior College at Fullerton, California but was not accepted. However, I was told to apply again the next spring and that they might have a position for me then. This I did and soon received a contract for the following school term, teaching in the junior college. Elsie and I were both elated at the prospect of a junior college job. As soon as the Corona High School term ended, we started to make preparations for the move to Fullerton. After getting settled in Fullerton I enrolled for some courses at the University of Southern California. Our new home was just across the street from a grade school where Willard was to start his schooling.

In order to help Elsie adjust to our new community, I encouraged her to join the Eastern Star, American Legion Auxiliary and Parent Teacher organization. I joined the American Legion and attended the Masonic Lodge. There were many social functions of the faculty. Elsie had always been very sociable and enjoyed being with other people. However, after several months in Fullerton, I began to notice a change in Elsie. She became very morose, despondent, and depressed and was not herself. She became very suspicious of her neighbors and withdrew from social contacts. She went to a very highly recommended doctor in Fullerton. He prescribed a sedative and she responded at first but later began to get worse. Her doctor thought she should have a quiet atmosphere where she could rest, away from the busy life of the city.

Her father lived alone on his ranch in Colorado and we thought that staying with him for a while would help. Her doctor recommended this procedure, so about April 1st we left for Colorado where she stayed until the following summer. We began to get encouraging letters from her and as soon as summer came, Willard and I began to make plans to go to Colorado. We left in July and went to Fort Morgan. Elsie seemed so much better and Willard was glad to be with his mother again. We drove from Colorado to San Francisco where we visited the 1939 World's Fair on Treasure Island. Elsie seemed to enjoy the fair so much. We then went back to Fullerton.

After a couple of months, I could see that Elsie was failing again. Our Fullerton doctor recommended a specialist at the White Memorial Hospital in Los Angeles. He gave her a thorough examination and found her very anemic and recommended a series of treatments. Since the White Memorial Hospital was a Seventh Day Adventist hospital and operated at full capacity on Sunday, I took her there every Sunday for fourteen weeks for treatment. At first the treatments helped but later seemed to have no effect. We tried several doctors but found no effective help. Since her stay with her father had helped before, we decided that she should go there again which she did. She did not improve much this time. Her father sought help from a specialist in Denver which did not help. Willard and I went to Colorado during the summer and the doctors in Colorado recommended that she not return to California for a while. I hired a woman to stay at the ranch and help with the work as well as to keep her company. Willard and I returned to Fullerton for the fall school term. I was able to get a neighbor lady to care for Willard while I stayed at an apartment nearby. I received letters from Elsie but they did not seem encouraging. She seemed to be growing worse. I continued with my teaching at Fullerton Junior College but there were trying times.

Early in November I received a telegram stating that Elsie was seriously ill and that I should come at once. I took the first available plane for Colorado and arrived there the next day. Airplane travel was much slower then. By the time that I had arrived Elsie had passed away. She was buried in the Fort Morgan cemetery near the grave of her mother.

I returned to California. Willard was only seven years old then. We continued with our housing arrangement and I saw Willard every evening. He seemed to adjust to the neighbor's care. They were very good to him. Every weekend I would take him somewhere to make him feel that I still cared for him and he seemed to adjust to the situation. Willard did very well in school. He was a great reader and got many gold stars in school. As a reward I purchased a small bicycle for him which he seemed to appreciate.

California has a teacher tenure law giving teachers permanent tenure if they are hired for the fourth year after teaching three years in a district. When I took the job at Fullerton, Superintendent Plummer assured me that tenure would not be a problem, but it wasn't long before a community ruckus developed. There was a Mr. Hale who had attended Fullerton Junior College and had a disciplinary problem. He had developed a hatred for Mr. Plummer and vowed he would get him discharged. He had considerable influence in the community and was able to get elected to the school board. Mr. Plummer had a contract for another year, but the school board hired another superintendent, put a partition the superintendent's office and let the new superintendent run the school. This caused considerable bitterness to develop in the community and at the end of the year all the teachers who had been hired by Mr. Plummer were not rehired if they did not have tenure. I was one of the twenty-six who were not rehired in order that they would not secure permanent tenure.

In the spring of 1941 I met Mildred Forslind whose parents lived in South Pasadena. She was teaching in Palm Springs and as soon as her school closed in June, I began to see her quite often. Of course, I was hunting for a teaching job for the following school term. Mildred secured a teaching job for the next school term in Corona, California. When I was offered a teaching job in Riverside, I accepted, mainly because it was only fourteen miles from Corona. By this time we were engaged to be married. I rented a small house at 3990 Oakwood Place in Riverside and moved in. On November 15, 1941 we were married and she moved into the house and commuted in her car to Corona for the rest of the term.

On December 7th, we awoke in the morning to find that our country was at war with Japan. It was not very long until gasoline, meats, sugar, and many other items were rationed. When we could get enough gasoline we often drove to South Pasadena to visit her parents.

I received a contract for another year at Riverside but the salary was low and I was not satisfied with the school system. It lacked organization and good management. In August I received a telephone call from the placement bureau at the University of Southern California asking me if I would be interested in a junior college job in Pomona, California, as head of the business education department. The salary would be much better and Pomona had a much better school system. I went to Pomona, interviewed with the superintendent of schools and was hired. So, Mildred, Willard, and I made plans to move to Pomona.

We rented a house at 924 East Kingsley where we lived for the first year. Willard enrolled at a grade school nearby. It was while we lived in this house that there came another member of our family, Everett. Everett was a husky baby. We were proud of him. His grandparents, the Forslinds, lived in South Pasadena and we would visit them although gasoline was rationed and we could not visit except when we had enough gasoline. I would sometimes dilute the gasoline with cleaning fluid, a legal procedure, but not very conducive to a smooth running engine. Most food was rationed and it was usually necessary to stand many hours in lines to get what food (especially meat) that was available.

Rentals were getting scarce and while the rent was fixed, it soon became evident that if we were to be sure of a place to live, it would be necessary to buy a house. In May 1943 we bought a house at 347 Adams in Pomona which was to be our home for the next eight years. Willard was now ten years old and was doing well in school.

I continued to teach in the Pomona Junior College although the enrollment had dropped decidedly. Most of the men were drafted and most of the women were working in defense plants. During my second year there the junior college was discontinued for the duration of the war and the building became a high school.

During the summer months of 1944 I took a temporary job working for a C.P.A firm in Pomona as auditor. My training in accounting stood me well and I worked all summer. I had signed a contract for another year as teacher in Pomona. By the end of August I was asked to continue with the C.P.A. firm rather than continue teaching. I knew that I had taken the place of a man who was in the navy and that he probably would return, in which case I would lose my job as head of the education department. So, after much discussion, Mildred and I decided that I should continue with the accounting job. The pay was much better and the prospects of promotion good. By January 1945 the principal partner and main stay of the firm died suddenly. The other member of the firm was very irresponsible and the firm's business dropped drastically. He later had to serve time for his misdeeds. I left the accounting firm and worked for another accountant making out income tax returns.

We were expecting a new arrival. On March 2, 1945 he arrived, another baby boy, Marshall. We were overjoyed again. Our family was getting bigger, there were five of us now and we were glad that we had a home large enough for that number. Willard was twelve years old and in junior high school.

After March 15th which was the end (at that time) of the income tax filing period, I took a job as full-time accountant for the Glendora Irrigating Company in Glendora, California, a distance of eleven miles from our home. I was allowed to buy enough gasoline to commute from Pomona to Glendora.

My intentions were to get another teaching job after the war. Then, in August 1945 the war did end. The celebration was much like that in 1918, the ringing of bells, blowing of whistles, and general noise making.

About this time a friend of the family who was working for the Internal Revenue Service was at our house and said that the Internal Revenue Service was looking for men and asked that I apply. I went to Los Angeles, made out an application, and took an examination which I passed easily and was soon hired, to be stationed in Pomona. The pay was better than that of the teaching job I had held in Pomona which pleased us. I liked the Internal Revenue work. I could be close at home and enjoy my family. I was a deputy collector at first but most of my work had to do with income tax.

In October 1946 my mother passed away with pneumonia and I went back to Colorado for the funeral. She had been ill for several years and her passing was expected. The funeral was in Las Animas and she was buried in the Las Animas Cemetery. She had been a wonderful mother, had seven children, two of whom, Clifford and Willard, had died in accidents. She had been an inspiration to all of us.

We continued to live in Pomona. The three boys grew and developed. We quite often visited with Edith and Ewald Hubb in Laguna Beach, California. Edith Hubb was the identical twin of Mildred and they had much in common. We also visited with grandmother and grandfather Forslind in South Pasadena. I continued to teach accounting in the Pomona Adult Education program in the night school.

The Pomona area had been plagued by an epidemic of rabies among the dogs and the city had been quarantined. One day Marshall and some other children were playing outside when a neighbor's dog nipped Marshall on the hand and brought blood. It was not a serious wound but Everett was thoughtful enough to inform Mildred. It was soon after this event that our neighbor who owned the dog called to tell us that the dog had been found to be rabid and that we had better see our doctor. The doctor advised that the only thing to do would be to take the Pasteur treatment which we proceeded to do[14]. Marshall was quite young but he was brave about it and went to the doctor regularly and took the prescribed treatment. It was quite painful and somewhat dangerous but we finished the treatment. There was no way to tell whether or not Marshall had actually been infected with the virus but we could not take a chance. We were glad when it was all over and we know that our boy was safe.

In February 1951 I decided I would like to transfer to the Agent's Division of the Internal Revenue, which had higher pay and faster promotion. I had completed about every correspondence course offered by the Washington, D.C. office and I had felt that I was prepared. I requested leave from the Pomona office and went to Los Angeles to

---

14 In the early 1950's the only treatment available for rabies was the "Pasteur Treatment" which consisted of injecting inactivated rabies virus and formaldehyde into the abdomen for 14-21 days. Today treatments are much safer consisting of cell culture-based vaccines and an immunoglobulin. They require only a few injections and are usually given in the upper arm.

interview someone in the office of the Agent in Charge. I was received and told I would be accepted later, perhaps in June.

About a week later I received a letter stating that I had been accepted as a revenue agent and should report for duty April 1, 1951. I was to attend a six weeks training course in Dallas, Texas. My duties would be the examining of corporate and individual income tax returns in the larger income brackets where the examinations would take place mostly in the offices of the taxpayers.

About April 15th, I took a plane to Dallas where I got a hotel room and started to get ready for the training. Everything went well until May 19th. At two o'clock in the morning I was awakened by the telephone. The message was from Mildred, saying that Willard had been killed in a car accident. This was a terrible shock. I had to make preparation immediately to return to Pomona. The instructor for the course was very understanding and I took the first available plane for Los Angeles, and arrived in Pomona the next afternoon.

Willard had a 1934 Ford. This car had a lock on the steering column that locked the steering mechanism and the ignition. Willard had had a date to attend a school play and took his date for a ride after the school play was over. While going around a curve the car left the road and tumbled down a steep embankment. According to the girl, she playfully reached down and turned the ignition switch locking the steering wheel and throwing the car out of control. She was only bruised while Willard was thrown out of the car and died of multiple injuries. She climbed the embankment and signaled a car for help. An ambulance was summoned and he was rushed to the hospital, but it was too late.

Willard was a senior at the Pomona High School and would have graduated in about three weeks. It was a terrible blow to all of us that one so young should have died needlessly.

Willard was of an artistic nature. He had won many prizes for models he had made of miniature boats and airplanes. He had a remarkable ability to draw and his notebooks were filled with drawings he had made of animals, airplanes, cars, boats, etc. I had planned to provide an education for him in some kind of art work.

After several weeks of vacation, recovering from the shock, I went to work at the Agent in Charge in Los Angeles, as a field auditor for the Internal Revenue Service.

After several months of this we decided that it would be best to move to some town nearer to Los Angeles. Mildred's father and mother lived in South Pasadena and were getting old and needed help and care.

We began looking for a new home and soon located one we liked, located at 2312 Hagen Drive, Alhambra. We moved into our new home on September 1, 1951. Everett and Marshall were enrolled in the Marguerita Elementary School within walking distance of our new home. The school proved to be a good one. They were both enrolled in the Cub Scouts and Boy Scouts and Mildred joined the Parent-Teacher Association and worked for the good of the school and community. She was also mother of a Cub Scout den. As cub scouts they went through the usual routine of ritual honors and began making trips to the mountains, desert, and beach. I became a Scout Committeeman and assisted with meetings and helped transport the group on trips.

I continued with my work as a revenue agent covering the territory of Los Angeles and the surrounding cities. My office was in Los Angeles and on the days when my work required me to be in the office, I commuted to work from Alhambra.

Mildred's parents continued to live at their home at 515 Grand, South Pasadena. The health of her father, Martin Forslind, began to decline. He suffered from congestive heart failure and in February of 1952 was under the doctor's care. He became very ill and passed away February 6th at the age of 83. He was buried in the Mountain View Cemetery in Altadena, California.

Mildred's mother's health was fair and Mildred and her sister,

Edith Hubb, decided to hire a companion and have her continue to live in her home. This proved to be a satisfactory arrangement and continued for about two years. Later her mother took an apartment near us so that Mildred could see her or phone her about every day and take care of her needs. Mildred's mother had several falls which resulted in broken bones and hospital visits. During recuperation from one of these falls she stayed at our home for several weeks. Later Mildred's mother entered a retirement home in Laguna Beach so as to be near her daughter, Edith Hubb and family.

In 1959 I was transferred from the Los Angeles Internal Revenue Office to the Pasadena office which made it much easier to commute to my work.

Mildred's health had begun to decline. She often had hemorrhages of her lungs. She had medical treatment which consisted of the inserting of a tube into her lung to deposit medication. Her health had been good during our stay in Pomona but now the lung condition that she had had as a girl returned. She had had her tonsils removed as a girl. As was the practice then, she remained in a sitting position during the operation and some of the infection went into the lower left lobe of her lungs. We had discussed surgery with her doctor but because of the risk involved we hesitated to have an operation. Finally about 1961 our family doctor recommended a specialist, Dr. Edward Hays. We visited this doctor and after and examination, he assured us that the risk would be negligible and recommended the removal of the lower left lobe of Mildred's lung. We knew it to be a dangerous operation but it seemed to be the only hope for her recovery.

I was not sold on the idea of an operation but she agreed to go to a hospital for treatment which she did. The hospital selected was the Maryknoll Hospital in Monrovia since it specialized in such cases and it was near the doctor's office. The hospital was about 15 miles from home. She went to this hospital early in March 1962 and Dr. Hays performed the operation. The operation was apparently a success. The first few days after the operation were critical, but she began to improve and soon seemed to be on the road to recovery. About April 20th she began to show signs that things were not going so well. Dr. Hays gave her extra oxygen which seemed to help her a lot. He tested her blood to see that there was no excess accumulation of carbon dioxide, a result of insufficient oxygen. Then he refused to let her have any extra oxygen although she repeatedly asked for it. It seemed that he was busy with other patients or thought that she had recovered sufficiently so that she needed no more attention and he refused to see her. Part of this time he was away on a trip.

Late one evening I tried to telephone her as I had been permitted to do, but the hospital refused to take the connection and would give no reason for refusing to do so. Early the next morning I telephoned my office that I would not be in and I drove to the hospital. I found Mildred in a coma. I contacted Dr. Hays. He seemed to think that it was not serious and said that he was sure that she could be given oxygen to end the coma. The treatment did not help, but Dr. Hays continued to insist that it would help. But it didn't. On April 30, 1962 she died. We had thought that she would soon be recovered and ready to return home. Everett, Marshall, and I were grief stricken.

Everett was finishing the first year at Pasadena City College. Marshall was finishing his junior year in high school. We carried on as best we could. My supervisor was very understanding and permitted me three weeks off from work.

I had already carried the burden of taking the responsibility for the household for two months in addition to my full-time job. The boys were helpful but had their school work to do. After going back to work, I would rush home and hurriedly get dinner for the three of us. I hired a lady to come in regularly to do the house cleaning. Saturday was the day to do the washing and other chores around the house.

During the summer Everett worked for a plating company in Pasadena and Marshall worked for a radio and television repair shop in Alhambra.

When the fall term of school came, Everett decided he wanted to attend California State College at San Jose. I knew it to be a good college and I consented. I went with him and helped him to get enrolled and settled in a rooming house. Marshall and I continued to live at our home. Everett had purchased a car and would drive home for special holidays, so that we were together at Thanksgiving, Christmas, and Easter. The Hubb family at Laguna Beach were very thoughtful and understanding and helped us to make a home. I found life very lonesome. I knew that I should let myself grow morose. I tried to lose myself in my work. I attended the Throop Memorial Church in Pasadena and tried to develop interests that would help keep me from sitting at home and staring at the four walls. I did all that I could to make the boys feel that they still had a home.

When the school term ended, Everett came home and got a job for the summer. Marshall continued with his work at the radio and television repair shop.

During the spring of 1963, I met a lady through friends in the Internal Revenue Service. She was visiting in California and had worked for the Internal Revenue Service in Georgia. I enjoyed her companionship and we grew to think quite a lot of each other. We considered getting married. I had insisted that she come to California to live, to which she agreed, but she still wanted me to say that I would live in Georgia. She had by this time returned to her home in Georgia.

Everett did not like San Jose State College and wanted to try some other college. I told him of the possibility of my marrying again and that the lady, Thelma Hampton, wanted me to live in Georgia. Everett was very enthusiastic over the prospects of leaving California and living and attending college in another state. I finally agreed that we should go to Georgia, so I sold the house and household goods and packed our cars and started for Atlanta, Georgia about August 20, 1963, arriving a few days later.

Marshall enrolled at Southern Tech, a branch of Georgia Tech. Everett wanted to enroll at the University of Georgia at Athens but found that the enrollment had closed so he secured a job at the Southern Bakeries for the winter.

On December 9, 1963 I was hit by a car while crossing Peach Tree Street in down town Atlanta and suffered a broken thigh bone and was in the Piedmont Hospital for 20 days and on crutches for about two months. The spot on Peach Tree Street was near the spot where Margaret Mitchell, the author of the book, *Gone with the Wind*, was hit by and auto and killed. We found the summers hot and humid in Atlanta and the winters were cold and disagreeable. The novelty of having snow on the ground soon wore off. We were glad when spring came. However, the heavy rains made the humidity high. We longed for the California climate.

I began to realize that my marriage was a mistake. Thelma had agreed to return to California with us but then changed her mind and asked for a divorce. This seemed to be the best solution.

Marshall and Everett returned to California in late spring and I stayed until August to take care of my affairs in Georgia.

Upon my return to California I rented an apartment. Marshall moved in with me and continued to work at the television repair shop. Everett worked for the Pacific Finance in Long Beach until September when he enrolled at Long Beach State College. Marshall enrolled at the California Polytechnic College in Pomona, California.

Both continued at their respective colleges until they graduated, Everett with a degree in Business Administration and Marshall with a degree in Electronic Engineering.

I held a public accountant's license with the State of California and during my year in the apartment I did some public accounting during the income tax filing period and earned enough to get one year's credit toward social security benefits. I was on the Board of Trustees at the Church and became the treasurer in 1966 with a normal salary. Thus,

I secured additional credits, which, together with previously earned credits qualified me for social security benefits.

After one year in an apartment, I decided to buy a house. Apartment living was too confining. I bought a home at 1104 South Cordova in Alhambra. The house was in poor condition and I planned to spend my time improving it and making a home for my two sons until such time as they would have a home of their own. I set about applying paint and wallpaper, getting new carpeting, trimming the shrubbery, and doing general repair work. Soon the house began to take on the appearance of a home. It kept me occupied and I enjoyed it. I planned to live in the house until I could no longer take care of it, at which time I would rent the house and move into a retirement home.

I had been attending Throop Memorial Church in Pasadena, California, a Unitarian church where I had been a member since 1960. I took part in the social affairs of the church as well as the business affairs. There was a group of adults who met once a week to discuss problems of religion, anthropology, philosophy and social conditions. I got great inspiration from the group and attended it regularly. It was here that I met Pauline Galvarro, who was a retired teacher. She had been the dean of students at the National College of Education in Evanston, Illinois and had retired. She came to California to be near her son, John Galvarro, who had preceded her to California as an ac-tor, but later became interested in the investment business. Pauline and I found that we had very much in common with similar interests, similar religious, and political views and opinions.

We attended many social gatherings together and I saw her about every Sunday. By January 1967 we decided that we should marry and we were married March 4, 1967.

It was not long after this that Everett announced that he and Arlene Crow planned to marry. They decided that April 22nd would be the day. After the wedding we held a reception at our home on Cordova Street.

Everett was working for the Safeco Insurance Company and was stationed in Panorama City, California. Marshall was working for the Minnesota Manufacturing Company in Camarillo, California.

Pauline's son, John Galvarro and family lived in Glendale, California. The families usually gathered on holidays at one of the homes to celebrate.

Appendix 1.

Poems Written By Adda Blanche (Doughty) Brookhart

LILIES OF CALIFORNIA

O'er the mountain crest we traveled
West to the land of white sea foam,
Where stately palms lift hoary heads
And flowers have all found home.

The mystic maze of motor ways
Urge us to wander free,
And just around the corner
Beauty waits for us to see.

The gold air and sunshine
Feel to us like rare old wine.
We gasp, at the wonderous [sic] beauty
Of the Bougainvillae [sic] vine.

We ponder the ways of beauty
When we see it all unfurled
In a creamy-white cluster of lilies.
"From whence", we ask, a dreaming,
"Came these? From another world?"

With feet held fast in Mother Earth
And no regrets or care,
They lift their pure white banners
And from golden hearts comes a prayer.

VOICES OF SPRING

(April 1929)

The fleecy clouds go floating by:
Above 'tis blue and clear.
A warble from the apple tree
Announces Spring is here.

The iris pushing through the ground,
The leaf buds on the rose,
Invisible voices all around
Proclaim the winter's close.

Voices of Spring that bring me
Memories of days that are gone,
Memories of faces I loved long ago,
Come trooping again in a happy glow
Like the lilt of an old love song.

TAPESTRIES

In my dreams I see a castle
Painted on the screen of time;
Just a dark and gloomy castle
Nestled on the River Rhine.
All aglow within the castle,
Candles, gleaming white and tall
And the tremolind *[sic]* shadows weaving
Tapestries upon the wall.

In this old enchanted castle
Come the forms of long ago
Moving in a stately fashion;
Slowly up the halls they go.
Ladies dressed in jeweled laces
Courtly knights with powdered hair,
And the candles casting shadows
Lacy shadows every where.

Then the murmur of soft music;
Clearer now, then far away
And the subtle scent of roses;
As back and forth the dancers sway.
Fainter, fainter grows the music
As it trembles down the halls
Tapestries upon the walls.

CANDLES

They have justly earned a prestige
Down through the corridors of time,
When the bells from ancient chapels
Sounded forth their evening chime
They blossomed rount *[sic]* the altar
With a holiness sublime.

Many sad and weary pilgrims
With broken hearts all torn,
Came softly up the dim-lit aisles,
By myriad footsteps worn,
Seeking and finding hope and peace
And strength to journey on.

UNTITLED

This poem was written after attending
the wedding of her son, Lester. 1932.

A bank of palms and trailing vines
A scent of roses too
A fairy maid in filmy pink
Soft notes of violin that sink
And tremble far away.

We stand a little company,
All silently we pray,
And then a maid in gauzy gown
With happy shining face,
The bride they say, and far away

The music soft again
Another comes and surely now
My eyes do cheat, I ween
My baby boy? A bridegroom now?
Where are the years between?

I hear the voice of minister
And now the plighted vows.
I see him sitting in the door
With chubby arms upheld.
The tide of years are sweeping back

And carry me along their track.
'Tis he, my stalwart, manly son
A happy bridegroom now, I've won

A daughter, pure and true
To cheer me down the sunset years
Make bright our path and dry the tears
Oh! Thanks dear God to you.

THE UNFINISHED ROBE

This poem was written after the death of her son Clifford in 1926.

Sick and weary and broken
On a bed of pain I lay.
My soul twixt life's terrible mile-stones
Seemed on life's brink to sway.

My darling boy had been taken,
Torn from me, snatched away
And I was left, weary and heart-sick\
With no desire to stay.

In the loom of life I'd been weaving,
The paterns [sic] were torn and spoiled
And I longed the world to be leaving,
From suffering I recoiled.

To patiently take up the burden
And carry on was right,
But how could I face the day time,
And how could I live at night?

So weary and weak and suffering,
At last I fell asleep.
An infinite peace and stillness
Into my heart did creep.

I saw an angel descending
From the clear cold blue of the sky,
As I looked and wondered and pondered
And questioned the reason why.

Over the arm of the Vision, I glimpsed a wonderous *[sic]* sight
A robe as fragile as cobweb and all the purest white,
Embroidered in wonderful pattern
And shining all over with light.

In wonder I watched the Angel
The wonderful robe unfold;
Eager, my hands were extended
The wonderful robe to hold.

With a look very calm and gentle
Just out of reach it was placed,
And I heard a voice say softly
While a light encompassed the place,

"Your work is not yet completed,
The Master has willed it so,
Your robe is yet unfinished,
You'll be called when it's time to go."

Comment: This poem shows very clearly her steadfast belief in a here-after. She believed that this world is only a preparatory station for the next world. She was very sincere in her religion and tried to practice it by helping others. She was not well in her later years and suffered con-siderable pain. Medical help was not as good then as in our present cul-ture, and religion was the only place to turn during pain and suffering.

Acknowlegments:

Publication of these stories was achievable with the love, dedication and boundless support of my wife, Marie, and my two beautiful children, Jessica and Ty. After all these years, they still listen to my stories. They read through this work, made valuable suggestions, and kept me honest. I am fortunate that my grandchildren live nearby—Jett, Kainoa, and Wilder—they keep me on my toes. I am a lucky man and I am thankful for them all.

I am also grateful for the staff at Outskirts Press, especially Dana Nelson. Their patience and professionalism made this book possible. And, finally, a special thank you to Terry Walters, friend and neighbor, who helped me to compile and edit this work.

Appendix 2.

Photographs

February 12, 1907. Arkansas City, Kansas. Adda and Lester at the funeral of Adda's father, Benjamin F. Doughty.

Undated. Portrait of Catharine Minerva Owens. Adda's mother-in-law.

Undated. Catharine Owens Redman Brookhart (seated) and her children (standing, from left to right): Ella Redman James, Newton S. Brookhart, Henry C. Brookhart and William Brookhart.

Ella is the daughter from Catharine's first husband, Simon Redman. The three sons are children from Catharine's second husband, James Robert Brookhart

Circa 1900. Adda's husband, Henry Clifford Brookhart and his horse known as "Old Fred" at his farm in Oklahoma. Old Fred was the horse he rode to secure land at the opening of the "Cherokee Strip" in Oklahoma in 1893.

Undated Photo - circa early-mid 1880s. John Doughty, Adda's uncle. He died of fever in 1886 shortly after arriving in Colorado at the age of 23.

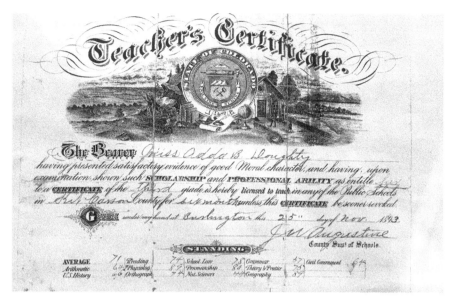

1893. Adda received her first teaching certificate at in 1893, at the age of 15 in Burlington County, Colorado.

Circa 1893. Adda at the first school she taught at (probably in Siebert, Colorado).

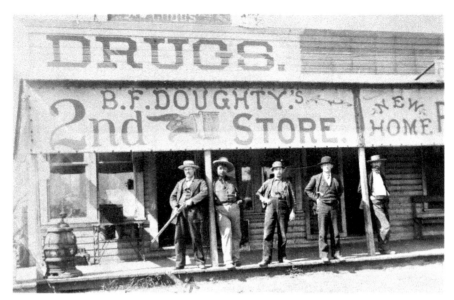

Circa 1900. Adda's father, Benjamin Franklin Doughty moved back to Kansas and owned this department store in Arkansas City. Benjamin is on far left holding a rifle. The other men are "frontiersmen."

Circa 1904. Adda and Henry Brookhart with children left to right: Clifford (baby on Adda's lap), Lila Mae, Viola Blanche and Lester.

Circa 1906. Adda and Henry with their first five children. From left to right: Clifford, Lester, Kenneth (in Adda's arms) Viola (in white dress) and Lila Mae.

Circa 1910. Photo of Adda's first five children taken in Tonkawa, Oklahoma. Standing in back, left to right: Lila Mae (9) and Viola (8). In front, left to right: Kenneth (3), Lester (10) and Clifford (5).

Circa 1915. Adda (left, standing) and her sister Mary Elizabeth Doughty Verhoeff (standing, right) and their children (left to right): Geneva Verhoeff, Viola Brookhart and Lila Mae Brookhart.

Circa 1919. Adda Blanche Doughty Brookhart with her two youngest children, Willard and Harry Adrian.

August 25, 1926. Clifford Owens Brookhart dies while working on an Otis elevator at the Continental Oil Company building in Denver, Colorado. See pages 66-67

Undated. Adda with her two youngest children, Willard (front) and Harry Adrian (Back)

Undated. Lester's brothers and Adda's two youngest children. Willard (left) and Harry Adrian, (right). They are pictured on the east side of the Bent County Courthouse in Colorado. See pg 69.

Undated. Adda Blanche Doughty Brookhart and her pupils at the Fort Lyon Military Hospital – Las Animas, CO. Her two youngest children were two of her students (Willard and Harry Adrian).

MRS. H. C. BROOKHART

MY POLICY

A more economical administration of the County Clerk's office.

Value in service for every penny of the Tax-payers money.

Prompt and courteous service to the public.

Care and Precision in Recording.

Undated. After a career in teaching and raising seven children, Adda runs for public office as County Clerk in Las Animas. This is a clipping from an unreferenced newspaper.

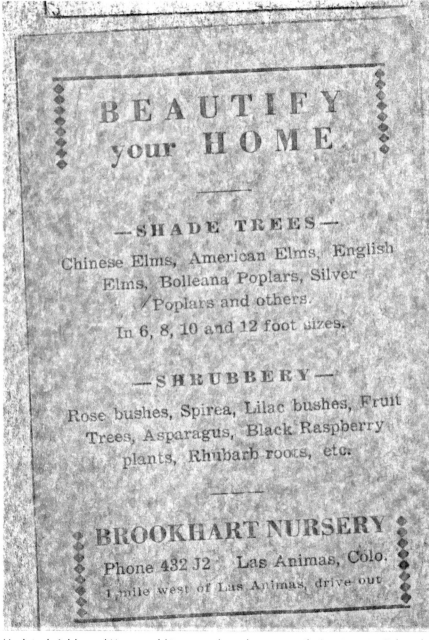

Undated. Adda and Henry sold trees and produce upon their return to Colorado.

Circa 1949. Grandsons of Adda, Lester's children, from left to right: Marshall, Willard and Everett Brookhart.

CPSIA information can be obtained
at www.ICGtesting.com
Printed in the USA
JSHW011144300323
39281JS00001B/8